# CONFESSIONS OF A SPECIAL AGENT

# CONFESSIONS OF A SPECIAL AGENT

## WARTIME SERVICE IN THE SMALL SCALE RAIDING FORCE AND SOE

### ERNEST DUDLEY

Frontline Books

## CONFESSIONS OF A SPECIAL AGENT
### Wartime Service in the Small Scale Raiding Force and SOE

First published by Robert Hale, London, 1957.
This edition published in 2018 by Frontline Books,
an imprint of Pen & Sword Books Ltd,
47 Church Street, Barnsley, S. Yorkshire, S70 2AS

ISBN: 978-1-52673-994-0

CIP data records for this title are available from the British Library

Printed and bound by TJ International Ltd, Padstow, Cornwall

Pen & Sword Books Ltd incorporates the imprints of Pen & Sword
Archaeology, Air World Books, Atlas, Aviation, Battleground, Discovery,
Family History, History, Maritime, Military, Naval, Politics, Social History,
Transport, True Crime, Claymore Press, Frontline Books, Praetorian Press,
Seaforth Publishing and White Owl.

or a complete list of Pen & Sword titles please contact PEN & SWORD
BOOKS LTD 47 Church Street, Barnsley, South Yorkshire, S70 2AS, England
E-mail: enquiries@pen-and-sword.co.uk Website: www.pen-and-sword.co.uk

Or

PEN AND SWORD BOOKS 1950 Lawrence Rd, Havertown, PA 19083,
USA E-mail: Uspen-and-sword@casematepublishers.com Website: www.
penandswordbooks.com

# Contents

# Introduction

Through a mutual friend, himself an ex-special agent, I first met Captain Jack Evans while he was living in Soho, about three weeks after his meeting, which he describes at the end of the book, with Father Andre.

I found it incredible to believe that this young man with his heroic record of fortitude in the face of death and danger could have so disintegrated as a human being. Here was an aspect of the secret war of commandos and lone wolves, fought as it was in the shadows, which had not been told. Captain Evans agreed to tell me his story, and I tape-recorded it in his own words.

I checked where I could for facts; but I had realized that it was not so much his experiences as a special agent, but the impact of war as he knew it upon his mind and spirit, its corrosion of his soul and the very fibres of his being, which were more compelling. Thrown into the maelstrom as a mere boy; a captain in the field, aged nineteen; and then, when it was all over, finding himself a peace-time misfit, fitted only for the excitement and hazards of the deadly destruction of war.

Captain Evans returned to France after leaving the manuscript of his story in my keeping. He was, he assured me then, going to teach at a seminary at Amiens as a preliminary to entering the priesthood.

I fully believed that this was his intention, and, though I did not hear from him for several months, I imagined he was settling down in his new life. It was only when the time approached for his book to be published, and I needed to get in touch with him for business reasons, that I learned he had, in fact, left Amiens. This was in April 1956.

I was most anxious to find him, and got in touch with his family at Suzanne, but his parents had no news of him. Their son had disappeared into the blue, and once again he made no attempt to communicate with them.

Determined to find him, the above-mentioned mutual friend and I combed Europe for him. Once or twice we picked up Captain Jack Evans' trail: news of him from Rabat, Morocco, that he was last seen on a bus for Casablanca, bound for one of the coastal ports, where he could get a boat for French Equatorial Africa in search of excitement. Another report was that he had left Casablanca for the Atlas Mountains, with the idea of finding some religious retreat there. I thought this was a possibility, since I knew that during the war he had been in touch with the White Monks. It was quite likely that he had gone to seek spiritual salvation with them. But further inquiries got us nowhere and we dropped this lead.

I had given Captain Evans up. He might be alive, he might be dead, but I felt convinced I should never see him again.

And then, on the morning of 22 March last, I received an urgent 'phone call from Paris, as a result of which I hurried at once there. Here I confirmed the information I had received and took a fast car to Vichy, where I found Captain Evans in a shabby little apartment, near the house which had once been the Gestapo's headquarters during the war.

I descended on him to find him looking harassed and nervy, chain-smoking strong French cigarettes. There was a sense of restlessness and excitement about him. He explained that he had not got in touch with me, that he had not answered any of my letters or inquiries for him, because he wanted to cut himself off from the past.

He was brutally frank about this, and to me it epitomized his mixed-up feelings. I tried to understand and sympathize with him. He did not show a great deal of interest in the fact that his book was being published, and was quite apathetic about the business arrangements I made on his behalf with a London solicitor.

Then he sprang a surprise on me by saying that he was now a first lieutenant in the French Army, and was due to leave shortly for North Africa with a paratroop regiment. He had come to Vichy because it was as good a place as anywhere to await orders to get back into the fighting, this time against the Arabs. "I am back in the old racket," he said, "and I am thrilled at what the future holds for me."

He then told me what had happened to him since I had last seen him, how the restless longing for excitement, to forget, was under his skin, and that it had in the end become too much for him. Despite the efforts of his friends at Amiens, his plan for a religious life, slowly at first, then quickly, disintegrated.

One day he just walked out of the seminary and caught a train for the south. After wandering about for weeks, he had finally had the chance of joining the French Army. And here he was. Not particularly happy, but with a purpose in life.

After we'd been photographed together, I got into the car to head back to Paris. The last I saw of him was as I turned to wave adieu to him from the car. He stood in the doorway of the dilapidated-looking building where he lived and waved back.

I do not expect to see Captain Jack Evans ever again. What has happened to him, where he is today, I do not know. But wherever he may be, his testament, unadorned and offering no moral, without apology or self-pity, speaks for him now.

*Ernest Dudley*

*Captain Jack Evans*

Chapter 1

# 'Would I Like to Return to France?'

One mild evening in November 1940, after working our way in and out of most of Oxford Street's pubs, two or three of the chaps and I found ourselves in the York Minster in Soho. The place was packed to suffocation with Free Frenchmen, soldiers, sailors and airmen, also Poles and other nationalities and their girl-friends. I had been there already several times, and had been fascinated by the proprietor's enormous moustache, the array of photographs of famous actors, actresses and sportsmen which decorated the walls, and also the odd colourful civilian types, mostly French, who frequented the pub.

It was just on closing time when I felt a tap on my shoulder. I turned around. It was H. … H. was about the same height as myself, very athletic-looking, with blue eyes and dark hair. He was in civilian clothes and said something about being at the Admiralty in some job. He was the elder brother of a boy I had known at school.

It was difficult to talk properly with all the commotion going on around us, and H. was with some friends, while my chaps were shouting at me to be quick and have one for the road, before the pub shut. H. glanced at my R.A.F. uniform, and asked me what I was doing, and I pulled a wry face and said I was absolutely fed-up with life at Abbey Lodge, near Baker Street, where I had been posted, and where I was doing nothing more than an office-boy's job. I, whose head was full of dreams of becoming a fighter pilot doing battle in the skies of France. H. gave me a sharp little look, and then he said: "Well, anyway, let's meet again and have a chat."

I said I would like to, and he said how about going to see the latest French film at the Studio One Cinema in Oxford Street? So, we made it for the following Saturday, at 14.00 hours, outside Studio One. Then my chaps grabbed me, and he went back to his party.

Next Saturday I was outside Studio One on the dot. A moment after I arrived H. turned up. He told me he had not had any lunch, and neither had I, since I had hurried to meet him on time. So, we went to Lyons' Corner House in Tottenham Court Road.

Over food H. listened with interest to what had happened to me while escaping from France when the Nazis came; how my parents were now living at Isleworth and how, though I was only sixteen years old, I had persuaded them to let me give a false age and join the R.A.F. All my papers which could have been referred to by the authorities were in France, so there could have been no check on my real age. I told him again how dreary I found life in the R.A.F., and that I was longing to do something worthwhile and exciting.

H. said he had been in France with Field Security and had been evacuated, and on his return to England had gone to the Admiralty. I thought his tone was a bit guarded, so I did not ask any questions about his new job.

It was over coffee that H. gave me that sharp look which I had remembered in the pub. "Do you really want to do something exciting?" he said. "Something dangerous?" He saw the puzzled expression on my face. "I can't tell you what it is now," he said. "But you are interested?"

I told him that he knew how I felt about getting into the war and fighting for France and all the rest of it. "I don't mind what it is I do," I said. "So long as it's a real job."

He stared at me for a minute as if to make sure that I meant what I said. "Wait a minute," he said, "I just want to make a 'phone call."

He went off, leaving me to finish my coffee, my mind full of questioning thoughts. He was back in a few minutes. "You've got yourself an appointment next Monday evening at 18.00 hours." He gave me the address I was to go to. "Just ring the bell and the rest is laid on for you."

I started to fire questions at him, but he shut me up and told me I would find out all I wanted to know next Monday evening.

As he was paying the bill, H. turned to me with an exclamation. "Good God," he said, "I have forgotten something: your age. Here I am thinking that you're old enough, but you aren't, of course."

I was so terrified that his remembering I was under age would spoil everything that tears of frustration came to my eyes. He smiled and patted me on the shoulder, "Let's forget it," he said. "You seem much older, anyway, and you have obviously got guts, and that is what's going to count."

We went to Studio One, but I never remembered anything about the film we saw, my thoughts were so spinning round with the prospects of my rendezvous the following Monday.

All the rest of the week-end I was filled with excitement and speculation.

I came to the conclusion that it would turn out to be some job to do with the R.A.F. bombing chaps. No doubt, whoever it was I was going to see thought my knowledge of the French language and the terrain where I had spent most of my boyhood could be useful to the people planning bombing operations over France. This seemed to me to be the most likely outcome of my interview.

Would it mean, I wondered, that I should actually fly with the bombers, or be sat at a desk poring over maps and aerial-reconnaissance photographs? I hoped fervently that I'd fly on the bombing raids. But it would be just my luck, I told myself, if it turned out just another job at a desk after all. Anyway, I comforted myself, whatever it turns out to be it could not be duller, or more dreary, than what I was doing now.

At last Monday evening arrived.

I walked along the blacked-out streets, dodging the shadowy figures of people going home. At length I found myself outside the address H. had given me. It was a block of flats, vast and impressive-looking, its entrance from the street to the courtyard within appeared to me to look like some medieval castle.

I went down the slight, rubber-faced incline, with a row of pillars on either side, into the courtyard, which was gloomy and shadowed by the dark buildings which seemed to tower above it. I glanced up around me. There was only a faint glimmer of light round the edges of one or two darkened windows of the flats. Beyond them was a patch of night sky in which glimmered a handful of stars.

I crossed over to the left and went through the doorway and up luxuriously carpeted stairs. There was a hall-porter in the foyer, and before I could say anything, he beckoned me to follow him to the lift. Without saying a word, he took me up and then along to a door on which was the number ten.

I could feel my heart beating quickly as I rang the bell.

Whatever I had anticipated I certainly did not expect the door to be opened by a major. But there he was, a tallish figure with a faint smile. I managed to pull myself together enough to jump to attention and salute. "There's nothing like that here," he said. "Come in."

He closed the door and helped me off with my overcoat. A major helping a mere A.C.2 off with his coat! The world had suddenly gone crazy. He introduced himself, and I gulped out my name. Though I was taken aback by the reception, I retained my wits sufficiently to notice that the doors leading off the hall of the flat were sound-proofed. The major led me into one of these sound-proofed rooms on the left of the hall. He offered me a cigarette and we sat down, and he began talking to me in French. He spoke French without a trace of an accent.

He asked me one or two questions about my parents and my home in France; but he already knew that my mother was French and my father Welsh, and that we had lived in a little village on the Somme, where Father had been employed by the War Graves Commission since the 1914-1918 War. He knew that my parents were devout Roman Catholics, that a year ago I had been sent to Cambridge Grammar School, as one of the teachers was a friend of my father, to study to become a teacher of languages. It was the school where I had known H.'s brother.

I told him how I had been back at home with my parents when the Nazis came, and how we had got out via Bordeaux by the skin of our teeth.

Then he asked me did I know why I was there?

I did not.

Would it be right to assume that I would like to return to France?

It would be right to assume so. I had only left France a few months ago and I would like to go back.

Under what circumstances would I like to return to France?

Any circumstances.

Dangerous circumstances?

Any circumstances.

The major's firmly chiselled features had relaxed while we were talking, and I sensed we were getting on all right. Myself, I had taken an instant liking to him and was thrilled to be speaking what I always regarded as my first language.

Then the major's face became grave as he went on to point out to me that if I was sent back to France I should go as a volunteer and entirely at my own risk. Did I understand that?

I understood, I said.

He asked me what sort of shape I was in physically. I told him I was in tip-top shape, I felt I could take on anything, or anybody. He made my nerves tingle with excitement, as he told me that my return to France was likely to be along somewhat unorthodox lines. "You'll be parachuted in," he said. Did I mind? I would be properly trained first, of course.

I was so excited I could barely answer him. He asked me one or two questions about myself and my family, and behind my excitement lay only the fear that he would ask me the one question I dreaded. How old was I? But he never did. Our meeting ended, and he told me I should be hearing from him very soon; meanwhile I was to return to Abbey Lodge and carry on as if nothing had happened. I was, of course, not to breathe a word to anyone, not even to my family or my closest friend.

I never remembered getting back to Abbey Lodge that night. All I know is that I walked on air, and that I missed being run over and knocking into people in the black-out half a dozen times.

I never closed my eyes that night, and the next morning my first impulse was to get hold of all the books I could on parachute-jumping and allied sports. On reflection, however, I decided that to start buying literature of this type might easily draw unwelcome attention to me and the activities in which I hoped to be engaged. From that moment I suppose my mental processes began to undergo the refinements appropriate to those of a special agent.

Although the major had counselled patience, I was full of expectation that at any moment a call would come from Flat No. 10. All that week I was on tenterhooks, which gradually gave place to a sense of disappointment and despair at the continued absence of news of the sort I was longing to hear.

Next week came and passed. Still no word from the major.

Sometimes I began to wonder if our meeting had ever taken place, if the whole thing had not been just a dream. I dared not try to get in touch with the major to find out what had happened so far as I was concerned, but I was tempted several times to contact H. at the Admiralty. But caution prevailed, I remembered that the major had warned me not to say anything to anybody about my interview. Anybody could include H.

And so, the days and weeks passed, and I began to give up all hope that I should ever hear another word from Flat No. 10. It was another of those frustrating efforts typical of the high-ups, who were running the war. I continued with my dull, soul-destroying office-boy tasks at Abbey Lodge, where the main topic of interest now seemed to be the approaching Christmas, with the prospect of leave, and the inevitable lashings of food and drink.

Just before Christmas I went home to Isleworth on a few days' leave.

It was wonderful to see Father and Mother again, and to hear news of friends and relatives who were in unoccupied France, yet I found it difficult to join my thoughts with those of my parents. The religious aspect of Christmas, which had always dominated my home at this time, only jarred upon my nerves. I found myself thinking over and over again that if Our Lord, Who gave His Son to the World, really loved us, He would stop this stupid war. How could we at a time like this celebrate the festival of peace on earth, goodwill towards men? The whole idea was utterly hypocritical. The mouthing of the priests and the pious attitudinizing of the Church struck me as being nothing short of blasphemy.

I knew it was no use talking to Father and Mother on these lines, it would only shock them and hurt them. So, I had to keep my feelings bottled up inside me, wishing I was back in London, still nursing, as I was, a faint hope that the major had not forgotten me. At least in London I could drown my sorrows in drink, forget my confusion of mind at the futility and hopelessness of the world about me and which so sorely perplexed my spirit, in pub-crawls with the chaps.

When I got back to London there was still no news for me, and so I joined up with another chap for a Boxing Day party with two W.A.A.F.s who were sisters, and who had invited us to spend the day at their home at Tooting. It turned out to be a pretty sordid affair, all four of us got very drunk, and the climax the inevitable amorous performance, though what exactly happened in the end I never knew.

All I did know was that he and I woke up early the following morning in the sitting-room of the girls' house. Apparently, we had been left to sleep it off, having missed the last train back to Abbey Lodge, where we were due by midnight. We got back to Abbey Lodge as early as we could, but on arrival we were greeted with the dismal information that there had been a check-up the night before, and that we were for it. Absent without leave, that was us, and we should be carpeted.

Sure enough, later that morning I received orders to report to the commanding officer, and make it snappy. Feeling desperately low and convinced that Life had nothing to offer me but disgrace and abysmal misery, I went along.

In his office the officer behind the desk gave me a narrow look, and then he told me in a puzzled tone, which he could not disguise, that he had just received a signal from the War Office.

It was top priority, and it said that A.C.2 Evans was to report immediately to Flat No. 10.

## Chapter 2

# 'This New, Mysterious Job'

Irushed straight from Abbey Lodge to Flat No. 10, where the major greeted me at the door as before, and he took me into his sound-proofed office, where there was another man, who was over six feet tall and always seemed to have a smile on his face.

This was Captain D., also of British Intelligence (French Section). To my delight I learned that I had been accepted for this new, mysterious job. The major told me first to return to Abbey Lodge, quietly collect my kit, and without saying a word to anyone, slip out with it and back to the flat.

This I did. I dumped my kit in the bathroom at the flat, and that was the last I saw of it. It was not the last I was to hear of it, however; three years later, when I was working behind the enemy lines in North Africa, I was to receive telegram after telegram from the authorities in London, requesting information respecting the whereabouts of my A.C.2 kit, with which I had been issued, but had omitted to return.

It struck me as being rather ironical then, considering the thousands of kits that were being lost, all over the place, with good men inside them.

At Flat No. 10 again I was told to take a few days' leave, though I must remain in London on call, and report back on January 6th.

I still had no clear idea of what my new job entailed, except that it was to be top secret and likely to prove dangerous. It appeared obvious that I should be parachuted into France as a spy and saboteur. One thing which had been made clear to me, as it had to others of the section, was that I was now a civilian. If the Nazis caught me, I could not count on the protection of being a uniformed member of any fighting force. In fact, if I was caught by the Nazis, I could not count on anyone.

Only myself.

I decided that I would spend the next few days with my parents. I had told them that I was waiting to take up a War Office job as an interpreter. I knew it would comfort them to think that I had landed myself with something cushy to do. It was not until long after the war ended that they ever learned the truth about me.

On 6 January 1941, I duly reported back at Flat No. 10, where the major introduced me to Lieutenant B. He gave me an idea of the sort of training I was in for, the type of courses in single-handed warfare which I should have to undergo.

Afterwards I went downstairs with Lieutenant B. There we found three others whom I was later to know as Edouard, Emile and Leon. Leon, I could tell by his soft, musical voice, came from the south. In fact, he was originally from Cannes, where he had at first been with Field Security. He was aged about thirty, and, despite the fact that he was of the south, where men are supposed to be the most excitable, I never knew him to be other than marvellously cool and collected. He was always the gay one, always telling us amusing stories.

Lieutenant B. led us to a huge car waiting in the courtyard. It looked more like a hearse than anything else: it was black and long, and the windows had been heavily curtained. We all got in and the car moved off.

None of us knew our destination, except that we were being sent to a special school as the first step in our training. We still did not talk much, but we kept our thoughts to ourselves; I was full of speculation about the future.

I knew that I should have to prove myself during my training, and, though I felt confident that I could tackle anything that was set before me, the chance of failure was present, and if I failed to come up to scratch what would happen to me?

Shoved back into my old job, I imagined, and to prevent that happening to me I meant to do my utmost.

As a matter of fact, I was to be given to understand, later, that failures from the service of Military Intelligence were not always permitted to return so easily to their former jobs. They might be in possession of secret information, and steps were taken by MI5 to ensure that such secrets could not be indiscreetly passed on.

I used to hear all sorts of rumours about special agents who when out of favour, or in disgrace, would be picked up and quietly put away somewhere for the duration of the war, where they would have no chance of divulging any war secrets that they might have learned. I heard stories of chaps finding themselves arrested on some trumped-up charge, and to their pained surprise popped into prison, until those responsible were satisfied that they could not cause any harm. Whether these were fairytales, or whether there was any truth in them, I cannot say. I was lucky never to be in the position of having to find out for myself.

There was still a feeling of tension amongst us as the car sped through the outskirts of London and into the country.

Apprehension regarding the unknown future still laid its fingers upon our lips. The gloominess of the car itself did not help to lighten our spirits.

It was about an hour and half after we had left London that we stopped. We were outside a large, dilapidated-looking house. Someone said we must be in the vicinity of Camberley, but whether we were or not was not confirmed.

As we went up the short drive to the house it appeared to be quite empty. We followed Lieutenant B. inside, and we soon found that the house was far from deserted. Within a short time, we were each issued with two battle-dresses, shirts, and a complete change of kit. Last, but not least, we were issued with second-lieutenant's pips, for during our training we were to be given the rank of acting second-lieutenant.

I learned this for the first time when Lieutenant B. handed me my pips, and I felt terrifically proud, and determined to make it more than a temporary rank. Those passing the full course would become properly commissioned officers.

After we had been fitted-out we set off once again in the black, sinister-looking, hearse-like affair. Our next stop was to be the end of the journey, and the beginning of our first course. We arrived at a most wonderful old Elizabethan mansion called Wanborough Manor, near the tiny village of Wanborough, about five miles out of Guildford. We were given lunch and allotted our bedrooms.

I spent an hour that afternoon roaming round the grounds: there were large watercress beds beyond the terraced lawns and gardens, with a great pond adjoining them. It was overhung with trees, and on the bank, was a tiny boathouse. In the middle of the pond was a little wooded island. Later on, the pond was used for underwater training by frogmen; relics of those activities are still to be seen at the far end of the pond today, although Wanborough Manor is now a pleasant country club run by a well-known actor.

Today the wonderful old house echoes to the voices of stars, society people, and amusing young men and women, unknowingly mingling with the ghosts of men who made a brief stay there, going on to training-schools in other old deserted houses, before facing dark unknown adventure and death.

The old house, covered with creeper, overlooked the Hog's Back, and, as I made my way through the orchard I could see the surrounding countryside grey and chill in the gathering dusk. I went along the path through the gardens, which were overgrown, neglected and sad. At the end of the path stood a garden-shelter, built of mossy and mellowed brick. I was just turning away to make my way back to the house when I noticed over the shelter archway the carved inscription: 'The garden that she loved.'

That evening we met the school's commanding-officer and our chief instructor. The following morning, we got down to work, and as the wintry days went by we became more adept at dealing out death and destruction. Lessons in unarmed combat, the use of small arms, revolvers and automatic pistols, and explosives. We acquainted ourselves with the craft of stealthy attack and swift, silent getaway, against the background of that Elizabethan house, with its beautiful gardens and orchards, slowly falling into decay.

We had almost no contact with the outside world - all our mail was first of all censored by B., then sent on to Flat No. 10, from which it was dispatched to its intended recipients. In company with the others I was conscious that everything I said and did was being observed and noted by instructors and officers-in-charge. I was never sure that perhaps even one of the chaps ostensibly training with us was not really a plant, to check on our talkativeness and discretion, or otherwise.

This atmosphere of secrecy lay heavily upon all of us, so that we spoke little about ourselves, confining our conversation to harmless generalities and trying our best to remain ciphers with code-names. I enjoyed all this tremendously, it appealed to my sense of adventure, and romantic lone-wolf ideas of fighting for France and freedom. The only cloud on my horizon was the ever-present fear that someone would discover the secret of my age, that I was only sixteen.

But the question did not come up then. The trouble about all that lay ahead of me, although I was blissfully unaware of it.

As well as instruction, we spent a great deal of our time planning and carrying out single-handed exercises against imagined enemy positions, or reconnoitring a certain vicinity. We taught ourselves to spot special features of the terrain which could be used as a hiding-place, or a secret rendezvous.

Many of these exercises took place at night, at all hours. Sometimes we were sent out without warning, with orders to reach a certain place, report on its precise location, distinctive features and so on, and we had to get back within a certain time. We learned to find our way by the stars, or, if there were no stars, by compass. I soon became toughened in body and alert in mind. I concentrated all my efforts, the full purpose of every waking moment, upon preparing myself to face any crisis or emergency. I would imagine myself in a certain jam, and try to sort out a way of escape.

One more week of schooling and exercises and then goodbye to Wanborough Manor. We were en route for Scotland, where our second course was to begin.

Once again, we ended up in a requisitioned house. This time it was a shooting-lodge, a large granite-built place, set amidst a wilderness of garden, apparently miles from anywhere. In fact, we were only a short distance from the ancient, picturesque town of Fort William, with its crumbling ramparts and overlooking glorious Loch Linnhe, beneath Ben Nevis, towering above it as if frozen into a solid block of ice.

Here our chief instructor was an ex-Shanghai police-officer, a specialist in knife-throwing and judo, and other refinements of swift, silent ways of killing. Despite some of the gruesome lessons he taught us, he was a gentle enough old boy. He was the first exponent of unarmed combat in the army.

We developed our knowledge of firing and ammunition; Fort William was provided with firing-range facilities for all forms of light weapons. It was here that I earned myself the nickname of the 'Gangster', owing to a certain aptitude I exhibited in the use of revolvers and automatic pistols. I certainly got a great kick out of fire-arms: the crack and answering echoes on the shooting range was music in my ears.

I became really hot stuff at setting my bullets inside the standard target, less than three-and-a-half inches in diameter, shooting slow fire at fifty yards, or timed and rapid fire at twenty-five yards. This sort of accuracy made me confident that I should be even more deadly at close quarters, until it was pointed out to me that though my target would be nearer, in a room, for instance, I might also have to shoot in the dark, when I could not see the sights. Or, I might have to shoot fast, with no time in which to align the sights.

So, I learned to shoot pointing my gun at waist level. It was not target-shooting at the standard target, fifty or twenty-five yards away, but it was the way I would probably have to shoot when the time came, with the man I was out to kill most likely only ten or fifteen feet from me.

I got to know all I could about my gun, and gained confidence in firing it by setting up as a target a piece of quarto typing-paper placed ten feet away. Raising the gun to eye-level and using the sights I would shoot my gun double action. I learned that by firing double action, which is the way to fire a gun at close range in an emergency, the gun would swing to the right. I practised so that it swung less to the right. The trick was to fire the gun without it swinging to the right at all. When I could do that, I knew I had reasonable control of the gun.

Then I began shooting from waist-height. This was without using the sights, but aiming by pointing the gun the same as if pointing my finger. I learned how to grasp the revolver-butt, not too low or gingerly, as if I was holding out two fingers as a sort of handshake to a chap I did not like. I learned really to shake hands with my gun. My grasp was high on the gun and firm. It gave me great comfort in the future, knowing that so long as I had my gun with me I would never feel hopeless.

Most fascinating, too, was this new plastic explosive, which we were learning about for the first time.

Plastic explosive was an entirely new idea and ideal for sabotage purposes. It was a putty-like substance, which could be moulded with the hands into any shape or size as required. A charge, to which a time-fuse was attached to detonate the explosive, could be stuck to a ship's side, or underneath a railway line.

We practised with dummy charges on the railway lines in the district. We got some laughs watching the drivers stop their trains to see what the loud bang had been about, and the faces of the passengers leaning out of the carriage window. Understandably our philosophy developed along reckless, uninhibited lines. We gave the nearby town of Morar a taste of this when its Home Guard Commander there rashly invited us to carry out an exercise against the town. The idea was that the Home Guard should defend certain strategic points against us.

We put into action the silent approach and unarmed combat stuff. Our opponents' tempers became frayed, until in the end the exercise became a brawling free-for-all.

That was practically our only contact with the outside world. As at Wanborough Manor we kept ourselves very much to ourselves. By now we were less guarded in our attitude towards each other, we discussed more freely our future prospects, our hopes and fears. It was almost invariably the present and the future which we discussed. Our pasts: who we were, where we came from, our real names and backgrounds we continued to keep to ourselves.

What the other chap did not know about members of the section he could not tell. Even under torture by the Nazis.

One subject which came up frequently for discussion was women. We spent many hours in the mess over coffee and cigarettes, our talk revolving round this fascinating theme. One or two, like Emile, would reminisce about the conquests they had achieved, and the philosophy of love thus acquired. Others, younger, adopted the line of wishful thinking. Marc contributed to these discussions in a practical way. He had been a commercial artist before the war, and now, helped by magazine pin-up photos, he covered the walls of the mess with life-size paintings of girls in various exotic poses.

Myself, I remained silent about the subject of women and love, and pleaded my youth as an excuse for my ignorance. I was quite satisfied to put up with any patronizing comments of Emile and the others. My mind was running along a single track in which dreams of women had no place. All I thought of was perfecting myself for the job I had to do.

We came to the climax of this training course; it was really the acid test which, if we were to carry out the next and final phase, which was training as a parachutist, we had to pass.

On the shore of Loch Linnhe we had first to jump from the third floor of a house, wearing full kit, steel helmet and carrying a rifle. Next, still in full kit and armed, we had to scale a high cliff by means of a rope, clamber to the top of a tower of heaped-up wood and jump from it. On we went, next to climb up and down a naval ladder, jump a stream, descend a precipitous cliff by a rope, and on reaching the bottom, fire five rounds with our rifle at a target a hundred yards distant.

Then, discarding our rifle and grabbing a revolver and hand-grenade, we dashed over a narrow plank across a ravine, on the other side of which we had to find a half a dozen hidden targets and, without slackening speed, fire at each one with our revolver. Next race down to the beach to a specially built boat-house. Here we must throw our grenade in such a way that while it blew out the door, the rowing-boat inside was untouched. We had to get out the boat, drag it along the beach a couple of hundred yards, and then push it into the water and row off.

Strenuous as this test was, we were now so well trained, strong and skilful that all of us got through with flying colours.

That night we celebrated with another of our parties. Next day we said good-bye to Fort William and took the train for Glasgow and Manchester. Our imaginations were fixed with what we were to undergo at the parachute-training school at Ringway, near Manchester.

# Chapter 3

# RAF Ringway

Even now, so many years later, I can still recapture the thrill of the very first jump I made that rainy afternoon at Ringway. I was to make many more after that, I was to experience that same apprehension and sickness in the stomach as the moment approached for me to leave the plane; that unreal falling sensation, like falling in a nightmare, followed by the glorious exhilaration as the parachute opens, the prayers to God for His care for my safety – I always felt marvellously near to God in that moment when I was held in His hand suspended between Heaven and Earth. I used to fancy myself as one of his angels sent to fight for Him as I glided safely to the ground. But none of these occasions ever quite came up to the fabulous first thrill I experienced on my very first jump.

Together with six others I had clambered into the lorry, and off we went to the airfield. We all of us tried to pretend we weren't feeling in the least bit nervous. We cracked jokes as the airfield came into sight. It had become familiar enough to us, the airfield at Ringway on the outskirts of Manchester, since we had arrived there for this latter part of our training, during those bitterly cold weeks in early 1942.

It had been raining on the day of our arrival, real Manchester weather at Ringway, and even now the skies were still greyish and threatening-looking. But they were clearer than they had been for the last three days, when we had done nothing but sit around the house, which was our headquarters for the Ringway course in our training, and curse the rain, and hope and pray it would lift so that we could make our first jump.

Now, the moment was near.

We got out of the lorry. We were already dressed in jumping-kit and we hurried across the airfield to grab our parachutes. We could see the plane from which we were going to jump waiting for us. The skies were growing heavy with imminent rain again as we strapped ourselves into our parachute-harness. It was bitterly cold as we came out of the hut where we had been getting ourselves fixed up, or was it our nerves that made us feel so shivery? We gazed up at the sky with dubious faces. Would we get in our jumps before the rain fell once more?

Then, just as we neared the waiting plane, there was an excited sound behind, and we turned to see an R.A.F. sergeant charging after us. Breathlessly he reached us.

"One of your 'chutes," he gasped, "it may be a dud." He went on to explain to our incredulous ears that it had just been discovered that one of the parachutes with which we had been issued was no good. At first, we thought it was someone's idea of a joke, someone with a decidedly warped sense of humour. But the sergeant's agitated face and the manner in which he started examining the parachutes on our backs, made us realize that this was no joke. Then he picked on Edouard's parachute. "This is it, this is a dud all right."

Edouard's face had really turned a pale shade of green as the sergeant, muttering how sorry he was about it all, helped him remove his parachute. Edouard – it wasn't his real name but his code-name, none of us knew the real names of any of us, only our code-names – was the first special agent I had met that day when I reported for training as a member of British Intelligence (French Section) at Flat No. 10. He had come straight from some civilian job, and during the past weeks he and another one of our group, Marc, who was from the R.A.F., and I had become good friends.

We had all been looking forward tremendously to this last course in our training, the parachute-jumping; it was to take three weeks. The first week we had spent getting used to our kit, learning to land without breaking any bones, jumping from a tower, practising falling out of the door of the plane, all the time looking forward with a mixture of anticipation and apprehension to our first actual jump.

And now, just when this moment was upon us, it had to happen that one of our 'chutes should turn out to be a dud. And after all the build-up we had been given by our instructors that there was nothing dangerous about it, that the stories about parachutes failing to open were only old wives' tales, that it was a chance in a million.

With all the delay about fixing up Edouard, still looking pretty green about the gills, with a new parachute, positively guaranteed to open, the plane intended for our use had been grabbed for another job. So, we had to stick around waiting for them to provide us with another plane.

To escape the cold wind that was blowing across the airfield while we waited, we returned to the hut where we had picked up our parachutes. There happened to be a radio there, it was in fact the only piece of furniture in the place, and with the object of cheering us up someone turned it on. Over the air came the strains of Chopin's Funeral March. There was a concerted roar of four-lettered protest, and the radio was quickly switched off.

At last another plane was ready for us, another final check-up of our kit and parachute-packs, and off we went and got into the plane.

The weather was still holding up, though it did not look as if the break would last long.

We were arranged in the plane in jumping order. We still kept our air of bravado going, but all of us must have felt pretty sick. I was really terrified that my parachute was not going to open, and I kept having visions of jumping out, and falling and falling. I tried to stop myself from imagining what it would be like, and if I should be unconscious before I made a hole in the ground.

We all wore a kind of protective rubber helmet, which some-what disguised our features, and the dispatcher who was with us, an R.A.F. sergeant, who was to direct our jumps, mistook me for a girl. This aroused great hilarity amongst the others, with various ribald comments which infuriated me.

The first to jump was Lieutenant B., who I had first met at Flat No. 10, and who was conducting officer right through our training courses. He was a friendly chap and had gained our full confidence. He was jumping first to show us that there was nothing to worry about. B. was, of course, an experienced parachutist.

The plane circled the airfield while we waited in our little queue. My mouth was dry and I could feel the perspiration pour-ing from me. For most of us, including myself, this was the first time we had ever been up in a plane at all. But, whatever nervous-ness I might have experienced being airborne, it was completely swamped by the knowledge that, in the next few moments, I shouldn't even have the security of the plane to sustain me.

All I should have was a silk umbrella held above my head.

The plane was now down to five hundred feet. This was the height at which we had been trained to jump, it was the minimum height for safety, allowing sufficient time for the parachute to open and to prepare yourself for landing. It meant that you came down pretty fast, but our landing-practise prepared us for this. Our instructors had taught us how to fall on hitting the ground, and how to get out of our harness quickly after we had landed. It had always been impressed upon us that leaving the aircraft was money for old rope, it was so easy. The thing that mattered was to know how to land; ninety-nine out of a hundred accidents to parachutists were caused by bad landings.

The reason we jumped from such low heights was that it gave the enemy less time in which to spot us, and to attack us. No one is more vulnerable to enemy bullets than a parachutist in mid-air.

Now the green light above our heads flashed, and we all braced ourselves to stand by. Then the red light to go, the side-door through which we were to jump opened. The dispatcher touched Lieutenant B. on the shoulder and he disappeared from view.

Next to go was Edouard, and as he went we could hear the pack which had held his parachute slap against the underneath of the plane. It sounded at first as if Edouard had got caught and was being banged by the slipstream against the plane. It was an eerie sound and my blood ran cold, until I realized that nothing was amiss. The others jumped one by one. Emile, a short, thick-set French chap with hooked nose and leonine head, was to go before me.

Emile was one of the eldest of us; he was about thirty, which is pretty old for this sort of job. He was rather boastful, regarding himself as being much more experienced than a youngster like myself, for instance. He was always saying what he would do and how he would react in moments of crisis; he did not get on too well with some of us, though personally I always liked him. Beneath his brash exterior he was tremendously good-hearted, and I always felt that he would be a good friend in a tight corner.

A moment of crisis for Emile had arrived now all right. Now he was being put to the test. The man before him had gone, and now the dispatcher touched him on the shoulder. Emile gave the sergeant an agonized look and shook his head, "I can't," he muttered, "I can't." The dispatcher gave him a terrific shove. Emile let out a yell, and as he fell tried to grab the edge of the fuselage, with the result that he went out of the plane the wrong way.

However, he had gone and now it was my turn. I felt as bad as Emile had felt; I did not want to jump, either. But I offered up a quick prayer, and as the dispatcher's hand pressed on my shoulder I jumped. After that everything happened automatically.

I kept my body rigidly at attention as I had been instructed.

For a time, I seemed to be lying on my back as the plane passed over me, and then very gently, it seemed, my parachute opened. From then on, the sensation was one of unimaginable bliss. First there was a tremendous relief that the 'chute had opened, and then a sensation of exhilaration, such as I had never experienced, as I glided earthwards.

The shouts of the chaps down below reached me, and I could hear myself actually laughing with excitement as the ground came up to meet me. I made my landing in strictly correct fashion, knees bent, body relaxed and toppling over.

I quickly released myself from my 'chute. I gathered my parachute and, swiftly rolling it up, joined the others. I had made my first parachute-jump.

I could not wait to get up there and do it all over again.

Poor Emile had experienced a rough time. He had fainted halfway down, and owing to his mode of exit from the plane had landed head-first. When I saw him, he was still semiconscious and badly shaken. Truthfully, he was too old to have attempted parachute-jumping. It is strictly a job for youngsters, and he was not a youngster anymore, so he was not really to blame for what had happened to him.

I had been the last but one out, and now I watched with the others as Leon, the last chap of all to go, made his jump smoothly and safely. Calm and unperturbed as ever, Leon had read comics while he had been awaiting his turn. Now he came out of the plane and made a perfect landing.

Except for Emile, we were full of congratulations for each other on our success. Presently we were all back in the lorry on our way back to headquarters, terribly excited and laughing and singing at the top of our voices.

# Chapter 4

# 'Jump When You're Ready.'

And so, on our way back from Ringway to our headquarters that afternoon, no voice rang out more loudly than mine as we sang and laughed, and I am quite sure that none of the other chaps felt a greater thrill at their success than I felt at mine.

We all of us, except poor Emile, ate an enormous tea, the tension of our bodies relaxed, the bow-strung tautness of our minds slackened. It was then that we found ourselves feeling terribly tired. That was one thing that I quickly discovered about parachuting, the hidden strain upon mind and body which took a tremendous toll every time of my physical and mental resources.

That night I did not remember falling asleep.

In the early hours of the morning I was awakened by a commotion in the room next door. It was Emile shouting. I rushed in to see what was wrong, followed by the rest of us, including Lieutenant B., whom the row had also wakened.

There was Emile, sitting on the edge of his bed, going through the actions he had performed that afternoon as he left the plane. Shouting, screaming at the top of his voice. He was, of course, fast asleep and experiencing a bad nightmare. Lieutenant B. woke him up, and Emile stared at us all with wild, glazed eyes, the perspiration making his face look ghastly and soaking his pyjamas, so that they stuck to his body. Then he began shaking all over, his teeth chattered, his bed rattled. Lieutenant B. and I gradually calmed him down.

Lieutenant B. was marvellously understanding and tactful with Emile, explaining to him that he was not to blame for what had happened, that he was very brave to have attempted what no man of his age ought to have taken on. While he assured him that he would not be asked to attempt another jump, at the same time he emphasized that Emile must not feel he had in any way disgraced himself.

Emile never did jump again.

Our schedule totalled five jumps. There remained four more to do, two by day and two by night. The first night jump was planned for the following night. But the Manchester weather stepped in again. For the rest of that week, and the early part of next week the rain swept against our headquarters unceasingly while we moped inside, miserably trying to pass the heavy hours reading, listening to the radio, or grumbling amongst ourselves.

At last the rain lifted, the skies turned from black to grey, and we were told that we should jump that night. We tried to sleep in the afternoon, though for myself I slept restlessly, and lay awake most of the time.

What would it be like up there, jumping into the darkness?

At long last it was time for us to go. We dressed in our jumping-kit, hurried downstairs and into the darkness outside, where our lorry was waiting, its headlamps masked.

Arriving at Ringway just before twenty-one hours, when we were timed to jump, we collected our 'chutes and got ready. We were not going to jump from a plane this time, but from a stationary balloon, the appropriate five hundred feet up. The balloon-basket would take only three of us at a time; there were four of us jumping. Emile was out of it, and B. was staying below to shout instructions up to us. One of us would have to go up alone; we tossed for it.

The coin did not spin so well for me and I was the unlucky one; I would have to jump on my own. Off the trio went. I went and watched them climb into the basket of the balloon, in the bottom of which an aperture had been cut out through which to jump. The three men arranged themselves round the edge of the basket and up they went, holding on to a sort of hand-rail. A red light was attached to the cable tethering the balloon, warning the jumper not to get his parachute entangled with it on his way down.

Up they went, Leon, as cool and unconcerned as ever, and Marc and Edouard making jokes, but really tense and nervous. Lieutenant B. directed the operation through an amplifier. The night was pitch-black, not a star showing above and a chill breeze blowing across the airfield.

Now the balloon was at five hundred feet. I wondered what they were feeling like up there in the bitter darkness, and I wondered how I should feel when my turn came. At least they were together, they could joke amongst themselves, and they had Leon's example to help calm their tightening nerves. I should be alone, with Lieutenant B.'s voice from below to comfort me.

B. was calling out orders now, his words distorted by the amplifier, and, one by one, the chaps made their jump. Everything went off without a hitch, but as they reported to Lieutenant B. each confessed that the experience had been more terrifying than daylight jumping by plane. None of this helped to cheer me up particularly, so that when the balloon had been lowered for me, I would have given anything for my trip to have been postponed.

But up I went, clutching the hand-rail, staring down below.

This was much more terrifying than jumping from the plane, this tremendous loneliness as I went up into the darkness, the shielded lights of the airfield growing fainter. At last the balloon reached the required five hundred feet, and hung there like a great ghostly ball in a sea of blackness. The basket moving gently to and fro; I held on to the bar like grim death, my every movement seeming to tip it dangerously.

I felt I could cut the silence with a knife, everything was so quiet – only the whine of the wind against the cable. I stared at the aperture through which I should have to let myself go. The perspiration was drying fast on my face in the cold wind. Lieutenant B.'s voice came to me through the amplifier:

"Jump when you're ready."

That I could jump when I was ready. I had all the time in the world to make up my mind. If only there was someone there to tap me on the shoulder it would be so much easier. But I had to make up my own mind, I had to tell myself to jump into the darkness. This was something the others had not known about, this was something I had not foreseen. There I was, stuck on the edge of that swaying basket, my time all my own. The effort to nerve myself to let go was almost more than I could manage.

I looked down at where the red light on the cable glared at me like the eye of some amorphous Cyclops. It seemed hours since I had heard B.'s voice. I thought I could make out below the red eye, faint shadowy movements and the flicker of a light.

I must jump now, I told myself. I must not wait any longer or I will never do it.

I steeled myself, I took my convulsive grip off the handrail, nearly fell backwards as the movement tipped the basket, leaned forward to balance myself, and threw myself through the bottom of the basket. The darkness rushed up at me, I could feel myself falling, falling like a stone, I was positive that my parachute was never going to open. My thoughts churned in a turmoil of terror. The red eye shot past me like a searing flash.

This was the finish. And then that sudden jerk, and I was gliding gently down. My 'chute had opened after all.

I had forgotten a vital fact. The difference between jumping from a plane and from a stationary object. After you leave a plane, its speed gives you a considerable impetus which carries you on quite a distance and you hardly fall at all before the parachute opens. Whereas from a balloon it's a dead drop, you fall like a plummet, you fall for very much longer before your parachute opens.

Once more I was experiencing that sensation of terrific exhilaration, of soaring relief as I was borne upon a dark sea towards the welcoming shore below. The cold waves of the wind blowing against my face, and whistling gently against the cords of my 'chute.

I landed safely, picked up my parachute in the darkness and folded it; then I rejoined the others.

I was tremendously thrilled to have made it, more especially as I had jumped alone, upon my own initiative. And I laughed and joked, almost light-heartedly, as the others pounded my back and shouted congratulations at me. Once again, we sang and laughed our way back in the lorry to headquarters. We tucked into an enormous supper that night.

The ghastly weather, not only the rain but the high winds, had proved disastrous to our jumping schedule, grounding us for all but two days of this last week allotted to us. Tomorrow was to have been our last day at Ringway. Now it looked as if we should have to stay on an extra week.

This prospect was a deadly blow to us, we were longing to get away from our dismal surroundings. We were discussing this ruin of our plans after supper, when B. put up the idea that we try and do all our remaining jumps the next day.

Three jumps in one day, it has never been heard of. Those in charge of our training appreciated that parachute-jumping exacted an enormous toll of us, physically and mentally. Of course, we were all enthusiastic about B.'s idea. Get the rest of our jumps over tomorrow and off to London, that was the stuff for us. We were confident we could manage it all right, and we were tremendously bucked when it was finally agreed that we could attempt Lieutenant B.'s plan.

Like the rest of us, although I was very tired, sleep did not come to me so easily that night as it had done after our first jump. After I had said my prayers, I lay awake, my thoughts full of what we had taken on for tomorrow. We had been in touch with Ringway airfield, and a plane had been laid on for us in the morning, the afternoon and the evening.

Eventually I did fall into a restless sleep, and then, a few moments afterwards it seemed, it was rise and shine for the hazardous day before us.

The skies over Ringway were still overcast and a chilly wind slapped our faces, as we hurried across the airfield to grab our parachutes. We were all keeping our fingers crossed that the weather, unsatisfactory as it was, would hold up. I had worked myself up into a mood that it could rain, snow and thunder; I was prepared to go through with it, get it over. The others agreed with me, but even our determination could not get us airborne without a plane, and the R.A.F. were pretty stuffy about bad-weather flying.

However, conditions stayed good enough for our first jump. This was, as usual, from five hundred feet, but we had to go out of a door in the side of the fuselage. When the time came, and the green light went on, the door opened. I was first out this time. I found myself sitting in the doorway with as good a view, weather permitting, of the Manchester countryside as anyone could wish for.

I did not wish for it at all – being able to see everything spread out below me like this made me feel sicker than I had ever felt before. The wind rushing past underneath grabbed hold of my legs hanging down, as if trying to pull me out of the aircraft.

The dispatcher's tap on my shoulder and I fell head first semi-somersault fashion. Once again, the sudden tug at my parachute-harness, the glide to earth. Once again, I made a good landing. One by one the others successfully made their jumps, and we were back in the lorry heading for a large lunch, our spirits high.

Back to the airfield in the afternoon. The weather still holding up, and our fourth jump to accomplish.

Once more we had to leave the plane by the side-door. But this time we were jumping in a stick, that is to say, the four of us immediately following one another. Our earlier jump individually had been largely to get us used to this side-door exit in preparation for jumping in a stick. To illustrate how quickly a stick of men could jump, the record at that time was ten men getting out in under seven seconds.

The afternoon weather was looking forbidding once more, but we got off the deck all right. Down to five hundred feet, while the four of us – B. was not jumping with us this time, but watching from below to see how we got on – formed our little queue.

The red light.
The door opening.
The green light.

The dispatcher's hand quickly rising and falling, no time to think, not a hundredth of a second in which to think, but out head-first after the chap in front of you. The parachute flowering, and seeing the man who had gone ahead of me, I had jumped number two, and then getting a glimpse of three and four, as they joined us in our descent.

Back in the lorry to an enormous tea and then rest until twenty hours. Our last jump was timed for twenty-one hours. This, too was to be in a stick. On the way to the airfield we were thankful to see that the weather had cleared considerably. The rain clouds were still banked low along the horizon, but the rest of the sky was clear, with even a bit of a moon.

Although we were beginning to feel the strain, and we were pretty quiet in the lorry to the airfield, the moonlight, as we went for our 'chutes, seemed to us to be a good omen for our last effort. Soon it would all be over, we would be back to a wonderful supper. Tomorrow, on our way to London, a well-earned leave ahead of us.

Now we were moving briskly across to our waiting aircraft, the same one we had used in the afternoon. Even the wind had dropped considerably, and the sky was clear. As well as the moonlight, stars dotted the sky.

We were airborne again.

Down to five hundred feet.

Our little queue inside the dark plane.

I was jumping first; I glanced back at Marc, who was second. His face, pale in the gloom and half-shadowed by his helmet, creased in a faint, nervous grin. He licked his lips and I looked at Leon, who was jumping last, his attitude nonchalant as ever, while he applied an orange-stick to his finger-nails. He caught my eye and thumbed his nose at me with a wide smile.

Once more the red light. The door opening, the rush of air filling the plane. The Manchester countryside spread out for us again, only this time by moonlight. A patchwork quilt of fields and roads, shadowy clumps of trees and houses in the moonlight. The terrible sensation at the pit of the stomach. The green light flashing, the tautened muscles, nerves stretched to snapping-point. The tap on the shoulder, the involuntary intake of breath, the dive head first at the moonlit patchwork below.

They make three white blossoms against the night behind me, Marc, Edouard and Leon.

The safe earth rushed up quickly in that last second of landing; we toppled over one by one, and our parachutes lay like fallen flowers beside us.

It is over. Our training is through.

All we have got to worry about now is whatever Fate has in store for us in the future.

# Chapter 5

# 'Cloak-and-Dagger Stuff'

Our commissions were confirmed as a result of having successfully completed our training schedule.

I was now a second lieutenant, General List. I wore no service badge, simply a War Office badge: this fitted in with my role of interpreter at the War Office. There was, in fact, a little more schooling ahead of us, before we were actually sent on our missions.

The time for us to be split up was fast approaching. This final phase in our training meant different schools for each of us, according to the particular mission we were to undertake.

Once again, a curtain of secrecy separated us one from another, none of us knew what the other's job was going to be. None of us knew if we would ever meet each other again, or if we did, under what circumstances. If we did meet again, it might be that we should have to behave as complete strangers, or even pretend that we were enemies.

While we were waiting for orders, the five of us, Marc, Edouard, Leon, Emile and I, stayed at the Norfolk Hotel off the Strand. By now Emile had completely recovered from his parachute-jump; he was almost his old brash self. Although he would never go by parachute, there were several other ways of getting him to France, and he was full of the plans he had, and the intrepid ingenuity he would employ. Now we were in London we also resigned ourselves to hearing about Emile's amorous adventures, in detail.

The Norfolk Hotel was an old-fashioned Victorian type of residential hotel. Marble-floored, with a somewhat genteel atmosphere of gilt and plush, it was difficult to imagine that it was in the heart of London. There was a quiet little restaurant; it seemed more suited to a spa for old ladies, and, though it was licensed, it had no bar. There were two pubs exactly opposite, however.

I used to wander down to the Embankment at the bottom of the street. I was always fascinated by the great river, with its constantly passing traffic, and the sea-gulls, making me think that the sea itself was only a little way off. One day, wandering round the narrow passages and courts which lie at the back of the Strand, I came across a wonderful old house in the alley behind our hotel. It had a balcony over an archway, and belonged to a London of long ago. I discovered it was known as Ye Olde Watch House of St. Clement Dane.

We were looked after marvellously at the Norfolk Hotel, everything, including all our drinks, at the expense of the War Office, of course. It seemed so strange that this quiet little place, tucked away from London's hurly-burly, was a home from home for desperate characters like my comrades and I. No gaiety or excitement, little likelihood of meeting any attractive women here. If it was that the chaps wanted, they would find their way to the Savoy or Ritz.

I used to go with Edouard and Marc for drinks at the Ritz, before a theatre or cinema. The Ritz was quite a place, the downstairs bar crowded with celebrities, actors and actresses, dancers and writers, some of them in uniform.

We had plenty of money to spend on drink and entertainment, since everything else was paid for, and it was never difficult for us to scrape acquaintance with all sorts of interesting and amusing people. But the three of us kept ourselves very much to ourselves, and always backed out of any invitation to any parties, or getting involved with any women whom we might meet. We would usually end up at the Savoy Grill to listen to Carroll Gibbons and his band. Here, too, it was always crowded, lots of celebrities coming in after the theatre. Marc and Edouard would sometimes find someone to dance with. I preferred to watch the different people.

London had endured and was still suffering from the grim attentions of the Luftwaffe, but night-life carried on with an astonishing gaiety. Many times, in these places where everyone seemed so amused and carefree, with rich food and plenty of drink everywhere, it seemed to me impossible to believe that people elsewhere were leading wretched, rationed existences, sleeping in shelters or in the Underground; that across much of Europe conditions were even worse, and torture and death stalked the land.

Not that I denied myself any good thing Life offered. I ate and drank with the best of them. I enjoyed the good living, the music and the wine, my taste sharpened, as was that of many people, by the ever-present knowledge that danger, even sudden annihilation, could be lying in wait for us round the very next corner.

I used to enjoy wandering about that part of London in the day-time. Fleet Street, the Strand, Charing Cross Road and

Shaftesbury Avenue; or Piccadilly, with a stroll through Burl-
ington Arcade and down Regent Street.

I was fascinated by the crowds. Although plenty of men and
women in uniform were to be seen, there were also those going
about their ordinary business, to and from work, shopping,
lunching, or drinking in the bars and pubs. Pretty girls hurrying
to hairdressers, or to meet a boy-friend at the Café Royal or a tea-
shop. It all seemed so strange to me that life like this went on in
the middle of a grim war.

I often had coffee at the Strand Corner House; I used to try
and sit at the same table and chat to the same little waitress – she
was a girl from Swansea. She would never believe that with my
French accent I had a Welsh name and my home was in London. I
explained to her that my mother was French, though Father was a
Welshman. Once she said jokingly to me: "I believe you are really
a spy in sheep's clothing."

If she little guessed how near the mark she was, little did I fore-
see that I should, years later, return to the Strand Corner House,
not as a customer, but in the kitchens, washing dishes, though I
did get promoted to working the goods-lift.

During all this time I had to report twice daily at Flat No. 10 in
case there was any news for me.

Like the others, I was now wearing a brand-new uniform,
which had been tailored for me. I was also paying special visits to
Flat No. 10 to have my measurements taken for the civilian suit I
should be wearing when I was parachuted into France.

This suit was specially made by a tailor who had escaped from
France. Even my shirt and underclothes were of French material, after the French pattern. I was very pleased by my under-
pants, which were of pink silk. All the clothes were appropri-
ately labelled, as if they were of French manufacture, every detail
attended to, from the stitching on of a button, to give every gar-
ment the appearance of authenticity.

It was a rigid rule that none of us must ever show up at Flat
No. 10 in uniform, but only in civilian clothes. There was a room
kept for us in a building at the back of the block of flats, where
we went in our uniform to change into an ordinary suit. We never
approached the vicinity accompanied by anyone, even another
member of the section. The greatest care was taken that no one
should ever suspect that Flat No. 10 harboured what it did, the
centre of a network of special agents operating in France.

All this cloak-and-dagger stuff was meat and drink to me,
and I was always most meticulous about obeying these orders.
It was proved most tragically later how fatal it was to relax this

security-mindedness, when one of our own agents carelessly revealed our headquarters' whereabouts to the Gestapo.

While these preparations went on, and we were waiting to be sent on our final course, things began to pall. I was longing to get into action, and the others felt the same.

In order to prevent us from growing rusty, and to keep our wits sharpened, we went on various exercises. For instance, one week found us at yet another of England's stately homes at Beaulieu in Hampshire. Here we amassed a wealth of knowledge which might prove useful to us later in the field. We learned everything it was possible to know about the formation of the Wehrmacht, its different badges of rank. We familiarized ourselves with French, German and Italian vehicles of all kinds, even railway engines. So, some of us achieved a boyhood ambition to become engine-drivers.

One night, while we were in the mess, some of us reading, some writing letters, we heard a terrific commotion outside. A squeal of brakes as cars pulled up, and the chatter of motor-bikes.

As one or two of us made to go out to see what it was all about, the door was bashed open and a bunch of German soldiers burst into the room. We were absolutely taken unawares, but we put up a terrific fight. I dashed for the electric light switches and switched the lights off. In the darkness I got to work with my unarmed combat methods, as did my comrades. There were plenty of cries of agony, mixed up with four-letter words. Somebody was bellowing with a German accent that it was no good our resisting; the Germans had landed along the coast and we were their prisoners.

We resisted all the more. It happened that none of us were armed, fortunately, as it turned out. For they were not Germans at all, but a force who had dressed themselves up, deliberately sent to test our reactions. When the lights went on again, the mess looked as if a cyclone had hit it. Although our adversaries outnumbered us ten to one, some of them had taken a bad beating.

On our return to London we were sent out on an exercise to Liverpool. Our job was to imagine ourselves enemy agents, and attempt to obtain all information that we could about the movements of shipping to and from Liverpool.

The obvious locale for us to cover was the water-front; the pubs, cafés and hotels. We split up, each working on his own, reporting each night at our own hotel, to collate the stuff we had collected.

It used to amuse me to go into a pub, crowded with seamen, some with their wives or women, the inevitable warning notices over the bar about keeping your mouth shut, because you never knew who might be listening, and by getting into conversation with a customer or two, buying them a few drinks, winkle little items of information out of them.

Incredible as it may seem, after only a week operating in Liverpool, we amassed a complete picture of the shipping currently entering and leaving the port. We knew what cargoes were being carried, their destinations, what convoys the ships would be going in, the sort of naval protection they would be given; and in one or two cases we even discovered the names of the Commanders in charge of the convoys.

All this information was vital to the enemy, and we proved how easy it was for Nazi spies to pick it up. Chattering in dockside pubs and cafés, listening to seamen talking amongst themselves or to their girls, never once did I encounter anyone who was not indiscreet, or in whom I aroused any suspicion. This despite my unmistakable foreign accent.

When we got back to London the lessons we had learned from our work were, of course, passed on to the counterespionage authorities.

Back to the Norfolk Hotel and routine reporting to Flat No. 10.

Then one day I was told of the mission that had been lined up for me.

It had been decided that as I looked so young, although, of course my real age still remained undiscovered, I was to be sent to Vichy France. Petain had conscripted youths for his so-called army, to work on farms or in factories, but the Nazis were sending them off to work in Germany.

My job would be to join up with these youngsters, with the object of inducing them to quit France and come to England to fight for the Free French. My destination was to be St. Étienne, capital of the Loire, whose main industry was armaments. The population was largely factory workers, who were very Communistic.

If I wanted to get a sympathetic hearing I would do best to approach them, not with a British outlook, but as a Communist. It was essential that I should be fully conversant with Communist propaganda and Moscow's line.

I was packed off in civilian clothes to a house which, so far as I was ever able to discover, was near Oxford – another of these beautiful old mansions I had come to know quite well. Wonderful grounds, surrounded by a high wall and massive iron gates, beyond which I was never permitted to venture.

I arrived late one dark night, so that I should have no knowledge of the route my car had taken. I was the only guest. The staff comprised a butler, a cook and a maidservant. Next day Professor X arrived.

Professor X was the only name I knew him by. He was from Oxford University and was a Communist. He was tall and broad-shouldered, and did not fit in at all with my idea of a wild-eyed, frenzied-looking agitator on the Lenin model.

Quietly, in his typical Oxford accent, he instructed me during the next three weeks in Communist politics, theory and propaganda. It was just like being back at school cramming for an examination.

Built in the old house was a massive radio receiver, so powerful that it could pick up any transmitter in the world. I had to listen to Moscow-inspired propaganda talks in French or English, and also broadcasts from Vichy, and then write reports on what I had heard. Professor X instructed me in preparing pamphlets, Communist fashion, in which Russia, the glorious Red Army and Stalin were extolled, never a word about Britain.

One of my contacts in St. Étienne was to be a man who ran a clandestine printing-press. I would provide him with propaganda material for pamphlets to be distributed amongst the workers. As well as trying to recruit young men to escape to England, I was to try to persuade the workers in the factories, whose arms output was now going to the Nazis, to go slow.

We also knew that the Nazis were recruiting key-workmen for arms factories in Germany, offering them attractive wages and conditions. Here my propaganda was addressed to the workers' wives and sweethearts, purporting to show them the sort of life their menfolk would lead in Germany. A lurid picture was painted of French workers always inflamed with liquor and surrounded by loose, sex-starved German women.

The maidservant was apparently a local girl; she had what seemed to me to be a country burr in her voice. She was a little thing, aged about eighteen, with very bright eyes. I hardly noticed her, except when she brought me my early morning cup of tea. She was always full of the day's weather prospects.

One morning she tried to make a bigger impression on me. She put down the tea-tray beside my bed, then she took two or three photos out of the top of her dress. "They're a bit warm," she said, her eyes very bright.

I thought she wanted to show me some snapshots of herself, and was referring to them having been between her breasts. Then when I looked at them I saw that she could also have meant the photos themselves. I had never seen anything like them before, though I had heard about filthy pictures. They made me feel rather sick. The girl was sitting on the edge of my bed, leaning over me. I could not believe that a young kid like her could have kept such things. "Got them from my boyfriend," she said. "He's in the Navy."

I was blushing bright scarlet. I pushed the things back into her hand, muttering something. She did not appear to notice my embarrassment.

"I thought we might look at them – together," she said. "Perhaps we might get some ideas."

I told her I was in a hurry to get dressed, and managed to get rid of her. After that, I discontinued having early morning tea, and I always locked my bedroom door at night. I had got Professor X too much on my mind to think about sex, even if the girl had attracted me, which she did not. And, in any case, for all I knew, she might have been a plant, out to test my reactions. It would not have been at all untypical for some bright chap at Flat No. 10 to devise such a means of discovering if my mind was one hundred per cent on my job.

Professor X found me an apt student, with a sponge-like facility for absorbing all the information he could impart to me. In fact, when I returned to London I left him more than half-convinced that he had converted me into a genuine Communist.

Back in London, now all that remained for me to do was to learn my cover-story. Then wait for a plane from which I was to parachute into France. I had heard that there was a R.A.F. squadron which specialized in flying agents over to France.

An agent's cover-story is one of the most vital parts of his armour in his lone fight against the enemy. It may mean the difference between life and death, when, as inevitably he must, he runs up against suspicion. He must be soaked in every detail of the character he has adopted, so that no matter how closely, how cunningly he is interrogated, he can never be tripped up.

Usually an agent assumes the identity of a living person instead of having a fictitious one concocted for him. This method not only gives the role he is enacting veracity, it enables him to absorb the minutest facts relating to it; occupation and background. For example, he can visit this person's birthplace, the place where he went to school, and of employment, he can familiarize himself with the individual characteristics of his friends and relatives, even with his hobbies.

There are no limits to which an agent must go in order to make himself one hundred per cent impregnable against the most searching questioning.

One agent I knew, a Frenchman, who adopted the identity of his married brother, took his brother's place for a whole fortnight at the latter's home, in order that he could not be caught out, even upon the most intimate details of his sister-in-law's physical charms. The wife was extremely pretty; could a husband's patriotism rise to greater heights?

In my case, however, it was not necessary for me to go to such pains. All I had to do was to be myself. I was going back to France under my own identity.

It so happened that I possessed two passports, one British and one French. On my last visit to France I had entered on my French passport, but I had come out on my British passport. Since my French passport showed only my entry into France, but no exit, my French papers would accordingly be in order, except for identity-papers and ration-cards to fit in with the current situation in France, and a story to cover the time when I was supposed to be in France, but which I had in fact spent in England.

It had been arranged with a contact in Unoccupied France, who was a farmer, that I could pretend to have worked on his farm during this time. Suitable identity papers and ration-cards would be provided for me by the reception committee awaiting my arrival. I was provided with a detailed description of the farmer, with whom I was supposed to have worked, his family and the farm itself. This was the only sort of cover-story I had to learn. But I absorbed it until I felt as if I truly had known and worked on this farm.

Everything was set. Now I had only to wait at the Norfolk Hotel for the phone call from flat number 10 to report, change into my French clothes, pick up the papers I needed, and set out over the Channel. It was late April 1942, and a bomber's moon was in the sky. The plane that would take me to France, one of these moonlight nights, would be flying with a bombing-force, destination Germany.

My plane would gently peel off over the spot where I was to be dropped and then return to its base. I was filled with excited anticipation. Whatever qualm I experienced, whatever twinge of sickness at the pit of my stomach, all was brushed aside by my burning anxiety for action.

Not only was there my passion to do what I could for France and freedom, there was the responsibility I felt towards those who had trained me. I was so desperately determined to prove myself worthy of their faith in me, the faith of men like the major, Captain D., Lieutenant B. and the others, who had helped and inspired me. There was also the admiration and respect which I sought from those who had trained with me, whose comradeship I had shared.

I was to be the first of us to go. This filled me with pride, I, the youngest, younger even than the others realized, had been chosen to be the first to go into action. While I was receiving my indoctrination in Communism, the others had been sent off on a course in radio operating, they were still away upon my return from my cramming under Professor X. They were still not yet back from their course, and in fact I departed on my mission without being able to bid them *au revoir*.

I got the phone call one afternoon just after lunch. Report to Flat No. 10 immediately.

This was it. As I replaced the telephone receiver I could see that it was misted with sweat from my hand.

When I got to Flat No. 10 I saw the major. "It's to-night," he said. "Car will collect you at your hotel at nineteen and a half hours. Be ready in your French clothes, you will be driven straight to the airfield."

I was not told the airfield's location, in fact I never knew. The major shook hands with me, and wished me good luck and a happy landing. Before I left I handed over to the major my British passport and other papers which I was not taking with me, and which, it was thought, might be of some use to another agent.

I spent the rest of the day in a fever of excitement. I tried to rest in my room in anticipation of the hazardous night ahead of me, but it was no good. I went downstairs and into the street, wandering aimlessly about until I found myself on the Embankment, watching the barges and tugs, the police-launches and other passing river traffic.

The river's surface shining in the late afternoon April sun made a mirror upon which I saw reflected the images conjured up in my imagination. I saw myself parachuting down through the moonlight into the shadows below. There friends would be waiting me. Would be, that is, if everything went according to plan. But if things went wrong, there might be a very different kind of reception committee lying in wait.

Time dragged.

I went back to the Norfolk Hotel to get into my French suit much too soon, so that I was left with a couple of hours still to wait before the car would fetch me. I lay on my bed, staring at the ceiling. I must have fallen asleep. I woke with a jump at a knock on my door. It was the hall-porter. Captain D. had called. I glanced at my watch, it was eighteen and a half hours. I had slept for a whole hour. I hurriedly put on my jacket and went downstairs.

D. had come to join me for dinner, and we went into the little restaurant. I was very thankful for his company, for what was likely to be my last meal in England for three months. I would receive news from other agents when and how I would make my way back to England. It might be by way of a neutral country, it might be that I should be picked up by a submarine. That was a bridge I should cross when I came to it. D. and I shared a bottle of wine, and he drank to my success and safe return.

Then the waiter came over to us. "Your car is here, sir."

It was another of those hearse-like affairs, black and sinister, the curtains drawn. D. and I shook hands, then I got into the car and off it headed for the unknown airfield.

My watch said just on 21.00 hours as the car slowed down, and I realized that I had arrived at the airfield. The car stopped, the door was opened, and I was led quickly to a low, shadowy building. Inside I was given jumping-kit and my 'chute. I was left alone to await the plane. I was warned on no account to leave the hut, in case I met any members of the crew of the plane. It was most important that none of the crew of an aircraft flying an agent should see his face. This was to ensure that, after he had jumped, in the event of the plane being shot down and any of the crew taken prisoner, none of them would ever be able to identify the agent.

I was to be dropped at one o'clock.

I seemed to have been waiting an interminably long time before the door of the hut opened and a shadowy figure told me the plane was ready. I followed him out on to the tarmac. The plane was a Halifax, and the engines were chugging over.

The dispatcher was awaiting me, and I got into the plane and sat on the floor at the back of the shadowy interior. The dispatcher had carefully avoided looking at me in the moonlight, and now, after seeing that I was all right, he left me and went forward. A few minutes later the engines roared and we began taxiing down the runway.

Now we were airborne. I could see nothing from where I was, nor could I hear anything above the steady throb of the engines. As time went by I guessed that we had rendezvoused with the bombing-force and must be heading for France.

A little after midnight the dispatcher came and told me that we were flying at a high altitude, approaching the French coast. Would I like to take a look?

I went forward with him, avoiding encountering anyone else, and saw the French coastline. All seemed serene and peaceful down there in the beautiful moonlight. It seemed difficult to imagine that we were passing over what had become enemy country. My beloved France, whom I cherished so much, which now lay under the heel of the Nazi jackboot. France, which I longed so much to serve. Now the opportunity to prove myself valiant on her behalf was drawing quickly nearer.

I said to the dispatcher that I had been expecting enemy anti-aircraft fire, but that everything had been quiet. Not even a searchlight.

"Don't worry," he answered me. "We'll get it soon enough."

I could not make out the bombing force with which we were flying. But the dispatcher had barely finished what he was saying when suddenly the countryside below me seemed to spring into an array of searchlights. I glimpsed the black shape of one of our bombers held for a moment in a probing finger of light. Then I saw the flashes of anti-aircraft guns, followed by the bright bursts of shells below us.

I watched fascinated while the searchlights raked the sky about us, and the anti-aircraft shells exploded in angry bursts of fire. Suddenly the shell-bursts were very much closer. My fascination at the spectacle changed into apprehension. The shell-bursts were frighteningly nearer, but we did not alter our course.

We sped on. I decided to return to the darkness of the plane, where I could see nothing of the danger from below. This was one occasion, it seemed to me, when ignorance was bliss.

I was feeling very cold, and I wrapped the blanket I had been given round myself and stretched out on the floor. I thought of my warm, comfortable bed at the Norfolk Hotel. I thought about it at length and longingly. I thought about Father and Mother, sound asleep at home. I thought of Marc and Edouard, and Emile and Leon, sleeping peacefully in their beds. The plane shook violently, and I guessed that a shell must have burst nastily close. It shook several times while we sped on, and all I could do was to pray, and think of those I had left behind me and wish fervently I was with them.

Then I fell asleep.

A hand was shaking me violently by the shoulder.

It was the dispatcher. He yelled in my ear that we should be over the jumping-target in a few minutes. I was to get ready to jump. My stomach came up and met the back of my throat with terror.

Automatically I strapped my parachute harness on, my numbed fingers fumbling, so that I was grateful for the dispatcher's help. The plane was flying steadily enough now. We had peeled off from the bomber-force, which had thrust on towards Germany, there to lay its eggs of death and destruction.

The dispatcher left me to go forward and check with the pilot, and I tried to collect myself, to brace myself. My thoughts were incoherent, but gradually I began to get a grip of my nerves. All too soon the dispatcher was back to tell me that any minute now we should be beginning the run-in over my dropping place. I tried to mutter something which was meant to be a light-hearted reply, but my lips were too stiff to form the words.

Suddenly the red light flashed above our heads.

"Action station," the dispatcher yelled in my ear.

The bomb-doors, through which I was to jump, opened at my feet. I took up my position sitting on the edge of the aperture, my legs hanging down. I kept my eyes fixed on the dispatcher, who was waiting for the green light. I tried to pretend that I was back at Ringway. That this was just a training-drop, that soon I should be laughing and singing with the other chaps in the lorry, returning to our headquarters.

I glimpsed the ground below, bright in the moonlight. We were down to five hundred feet all right, and I could see the ground clearly. We were over what I knew were deserted fields, with clumps of trees throwing dark shadows across the ground, but I could see no sign of movement below, no flicker of light signalling us. I fixed my eyes again upon the dispatcher's face. He was frowning now, and glancing uncertainly at where the green light should flash.

There was no green light.

My legs and feet were becoming chilled through in the icy wind that whipped up into the aircraft. My thighs and hips were stiff. My arms which were gripping the edges of the opening were aching with the strain.

We circled round the dropping-area. The plane began its run-in again.

Still no green light.

The plane kept circling, it kept circling for an hour. Never was there any movement, any sign of anyone awaiting us down there, in the shadows. No signal light to reassure us that all was well. That there were friends waiting for me. Still we circled.

I looked at the dispatcher as there came a movement from the darkness of the plane and one of the crew appeared. He spoke urgently into the dispatcher's ear. The dispatcher was scowling; then he nodded and waved at me to get back in the plane.

Something had gone wrong.

I was not going to jump after all. Not yet. A wave of mingled relief and bewilderment swept over me as I tried to lever myself back into the plane, but my tired arms did not respond. The slip-stream was trying to drag me out of the plane. The dispatcher was shouting at me, though I could not catch the words. Panic seized me as I struggled to heave myself up; I had a terrifying vision of being unable to save myself from slipping through the bomb-doors before the dispatcher could come to my aid. I threw him an agonized look, but he did not seem to understand my predicament, he kept waving me back and shouting.

I made a supreme effort, the perspiration pouring down my face, impelled myself upwards and backwards into the plane and collapsed on the floor, gasping for breath like a fish stranded on dry land. The dispatcher bent and shouted in my ears that my jump was off, no signal from below, no signs of any reception committee there to welcome me.

Somehow, somewhere along the line, the plan had gone astray. I was so overcome by exhaustion as a result of the strain of it all that I barely grasped what he was saying. All I knew was that any relief I had felt now gave place to exhausted disappointment before I drifted away into sleep.

I slept all the way back.

# Chapter 6

# Captain Appleyard

The same black, hearse-like car was awaiting me when I got back to the airfield, which I had left a few hours previously. A dreadful sense of anticlimax pressed down upon me as I made my way wearily to the car. The airfield had an unreal, dreamlike appearance in the chill darkness of the early morning. My head rang with questions, but I knew that I should stand no chance of getting any satisfactory answers until I got back to Flat No. 10. No one at the airfield would know anything. None of the Halifax's crew either would have any information to give me; all that had happened, so far as they were concerned, was that receiving no signal from the ground and after circling the area for an hour they had acted on instructions and headed back home.

It was not the first time that a trip such as the one I had been on had ended abortively; there could be several reasons to account for what had happened. The reception committee which was to have been there to meet me might never have got to the place where I was to land. They might have received a tip-off that the Nazis knew that an agent was expected; or they might have found enemy personnel in the vicinity when they arrived, and been forced to lie low, or beat a quiet retreat. Any of these, or other possibilities, could have been responsible for the absence of the reception committee.

I dozed fitfully in the car back to London, waking up every now and then in the middle of crazy, terror-filled dreams. Arriving at the Norfolk Hotel, to which the driver had orders to return me, I went straight to my bedroom. I hardly had enough energy left to get out of my clothes, and I fell into bed and into a deep sleep of utter exhaustion.

Next morning at mid-day I reported at Flat No. 10.

The moment I entered Flat No. 10 I sensed that something was wrong; nor was it, I felt, to do only with my trip of the night before. I was not kept waiting long before I discovered what the trouble was. It was that damned British passport of mine which I had given the major. It had completely escaped my mind that it bore my real age. The fact had been spotted that morning, and both the major and Captain D. had been a bit shaken by the revelation that I was only sixteen. When they told me about it and I replied that I should, in fact, be seventeen within a few weeks, it was received with little enthusiasm. I was told there and then that the French Section would have to wash its hands of me.

It seemed that I was far too young to be expected to endure torture by the Gestapo, that I simply could not be expected to possess this kind of stamina and guts required by a special agent. I hotly disputed this point of view, I could take anything the Nazis could hand out, I answered, as well as if not better than mature men. But it was no use, my British passport was raised in my face. I was too young.

I finally ended up that afternoon at an office at MI5. Here an officer in Security reduced me to tears. "You've behaved like a rash little fool," he told me. "As soon as we can think what's best to be done with you, you'll hear from us. Meantime, you're kicked out of the French Section, and you'd better not move from your hotel, until you're told."

On my way back to the hotel I realized the enormity of my offence. I had come into the possession of important secrets which, at my so-called irresponsible age, I ought never to have known. In other words, I knew much more than was good for me, and from the point of view of Military Intelligence, I could prove a source of embarrassment, even danger.

What was going to happen to me? That was the question running round my brain the rest of that day, and throughout most of a sleepless night.

If only there had been someone to talk to, Marc or Edouard, or any of the others. But they were all still away on their radio course.

I had visions of being packed off to some prison, and kept there for the war's duration, in order to make certain that I should not, in a moment of indiscretion, spill any beans about the activities in which I had been engaged. What an ignominiously dismal end to all my dreams of serving the cause of France! How should I ever hold up my head again?

All that I could do through that long, restless night was to pray to God as I had never prayed before, for His help. After breakfast the next morning I received a 'phone call to report at Flat No. 10 at 11.00 hours.

I was filled with bitter despair, mingled with most fearful imaginings. I thought of a Roman Catholic church, which I had visited several times before, on my way to and from Flat No. 10. Straight away I hurried off to it, where I remained for the next two hours, continuing to pray that something would happen which would allow me to continue in the fight against the Nazis.

I arrived at Flat No. 10 in a more settled frame of mind, resigned to accept whatever was handed out to me. The major saw me at once, and I detected a twinkle at the back of his eyes, which had not been there the day before.

"We have decided not to have you shot after all," he said. "In fact, there is quite a chance that you may be able to stay on here." My heart leapt with joy, and he went on: "Can't tell you any more for the moment. Better hang around at the Norfolk and you'll hear from us in a few days."

He shook hands with me and pushed me out of the office, and as I left I was weeping again. This time they were tears of happiness. On my way back to the hotel I looked in once more at the church to thank God for answering my prayers.

It was at the beginning of the following week that I reported again at Flat No. 10.

I arrived there full of excited speculation. This time Captain D. showed me into a sound-proofed room in which two men were waiting for me. The elder one, who wore a moustache, carried a bowler hat and an umbrella. He was wearing a black coat and striped trousers, and looked as if he had just come up from the City. He introduced himself as Major March-Phillips. The other chap with him was very much younger; I think he was the handsomest man I ever saw, with blonde hair and blue eyes, and the figure of an athlete. He was dressed casually in a pair of flannels and sports-jacket. He introduced himself as Captain Appleyard.

March-Phillips and Appleyard gave me some idea of the job they had been doing, and their future plans. They had been employed in West Africa as sort of commandos. They operated under the Chief of Combined Operations, Admiral Lord Mountbatten. "We take orders direct from the C.-in-C. himself," Appleyard said. "No red tape, no frustrating brass-hats to get in the way. Just pure operations, and success depends on you, and you alone."

Appleyard and March-Phillips and their raiding-party had in fact done a fine job along the West African coast. They had attacked enemy shipping and captured crews and vessels. In an old Brixham trawler, which they had specially converted, they had nosed their way into the river deltas along the Atlantic seaboard of Vichy West Africa, which were being used as refuelling depots for German U-Boats.

With all the experience they had gained in this type of lone-wolf warfare, they had been recalled to England to set up a new

Commando force, which would operate in small groups along the French coast, using fast motor-vessels and landing-craft specially designed by them. They were recruiting the nucleus for this new branch of Special Services Command, and I had been recommended to them by the major as a useful type, despite the fact that I was under-age.

Appleyard himself was only in his early twenties, and he smiled at me when the question of my age cropped up. "This is a job for youngsters," he said. "You can speak French, you've had some training, parachute-jumping and so on, and by the time we've finished with you, we'll have put years on you all right." We all laughed.

I was told that I would need a course of intensive training in the technique of Combined Operations raids, the object of which was to harass the Nazis so that they would never know where and when to expect a blow. And, more practically, to obtain prisoners and information; to sabotage airfields and naval and military installations. To all this would be added the important propaganda effect upon the French, longing to overthrow the invaders.

To this end the aim would be to become adept in handling boats in all kinds of weather and under fire, in navigating in the blackest night, the stormiest sea, in and out of rocky bays. We would be trained to develop our initiative and self-reliance. There would be no rules and regulations, or punishments. If a chap let the side down, he was out. That was all there was to it.

It all sounded absolutely terrific to me. I was thrilled by March-Phillips' and Appleyard's enthusiasm and ideas for these audacious thrusts out of the night, carrying the war into the enemy's camp. I could not wait to join them.

As in the case of the job from which I had been kicked out, secrecy was the watchword. I left March-Phillips and Appleyard with orders to wait at the Norfolk Hotel for the word to report for training. There were hopes of taking over a house near the Dorset coast as training and actual operations headquarters.

On my way out of the flat I looked in to tell Captain D. of my new job, and how thrilled I was about it. "You're damned lucky," he said. "They're two of the very best; you wanted excitement, you'll get it with them."

I left walking on air.

During the next few days, while I was waiting to hear again from March-Phillips and Appleyard, the chaps returned from their radio-instruction courses. But it was only a matter of a day or two before, one by one, each went off to study his cover-story, immediately prior to going out on his mission.

They were all pretty tensed-up, and, as I had been, anxious to get it over with. All except Leon, of course, who was imperturbable as ever; he might have been going away for a weekend at Brighton, for all the emotion he showed. I was to meet none of them again, except Emile, for a long time.

Leon, I never did see any more, after I watched him turn and wave a nonchalant *au revoir* at me, as he went out of the hotel one morning. I heard long afterwards what happened to him, how his mission took him back to the South he loved so much.

With typically cool audacity he walked into a Nazi Naval school at Toulon, which was training U-Boat Commanders. This was at the time when the Allies had stepped up the war against the U-Boats, which were playing havoc with our shipping. Leon picked a day when the school was full of cadets, passing out to take up their duties. Posing as a press photographer, he arrived on the scene carrying what was apparently his camera. At the crucial moment he clicked the shutter and there was a terrific explosion. Among those potential U-Boat Commanders who were blown to bits was Leon himself.

One morning I received the message for which I had been so impatiently waiting.

I was to report at once, with all my kit, at an address in Whitehall. My taxi stopped outside an old grey building half-way down from Trafalgar Square, just by the familiar gateway to Horse Guards Parade. I went through a small, dark door and upstairs. As I went up I could smell the stables of the Horse Guards; it was very strong.

The room in which I found myself was crowded, and the aroma of tobacco smoke from one or two pipes mingled with the smell of horses from below. The room seemed to be more of a stable loft than an office. There was a desk in a corner and telephones, but there was no carpet on the bare boards, and from some pegs along one wall hung some harness. Appleyard was there, but March-Phillips wasn't. He was, Appleyard told me, trying to obtain some sea-going craft from the Admiralty.

Among those I was introduced to was a hefty chap with a moustache and a thick head of hair, who was Captain Graham Hayes, and Captain the Lord Howard of Penrith, who was very charming; I took to him right away. There was also a Lieutenant de G. from the French Navy. He and I were to become very close friends. He spoke no English, so stuck to me like a limpet wherever we went. There was a terrific atmosphere of excitement in the room, while we joked and laughed together.

Then Appleyard told us that we were off right away to Dorset. He and March-Phillips had managed to get hold of an old house about five miles away from a place called Blandford. And so, we all fell into taxis with our kit and got to the station to catch the train for Dorchester, where we should be met by cars to take us to our new headquarters.

Once again it was another stately home of England, a glorious Tudor mansion, somewhat crumbling and dilapidated. All the rooms had very small mullioned windows, and typically enough it possessed only one bathroom, so that there used to be a free-for-all among us every morning as to who should get in first. The house stood in its own grounds, beautiful gardens and a park, on the other side of which was a farm, also belonging to the house. Some of those who had joined us were already there when we arrived.

The first few days we spent sorting ourselves out, which included finding a little inn about ten minutes away called the World's End. They brewed their own cider here, and we became regular customers. Then we got down to work in earnest.

We laid out an assault course with which I had already become familiar from the shores of Loch Linnhe, in the park; and we set up a revolver-range at the back of the old house. So that I was once again able to enjoy the feel of lethal automatics and revolvers in my hand, to revel in the crack and boom of firing practice, and to live up to my nickname, the 'Gangster'.

I added to my knowledge of small firearms; we were taught how to use those of German and Italian type. We should not be able to take much in the way of arms on our raids and might have to use any of the enemy's we could lay our hands on.

Although the old house had been requisitioned by us, the owner had not left. She was a woman in her sixties, and she had shut herself off from the rest of us in the house. We got occasional glimpses of her, but that was all. I used often to wonder what she must think of this horde of men, who had descended on the place with their high spirits and bent upon such desperate activities.

Over at Poole Harbour we practised landing and re-embarking in the small boats we should be using for our swift, silent thrusts from the sea; other days with instructors absorbing the technique of all-in fighting, from them we learned to think in terms of kill or be killed. We learned to fight with or without weapons. We learned how to creep up upon a man in the dark and kill him silently and swiftly.

Ruthlessness, speed and brutality, these were our watchwords. It did not matter what we did to our enemy so long as we did it thoroughly and quickly, before he had time to do it to us.

We learned a mixture of judo, using blows with the edge of the hand, and all-in brawling, ranging from kicks and knee-jabs to eye-gouging and mouth-tearing. We learned how best to break a man's neck, or how to strangle him from behind, or from the front.

Our training also included the use of the knife as an offensive weapon; we were taught how to slash and stab from all angles. This method was particularly suitable when dealing with sentries. We learned how to creep upon a sentry out of the darkness and leap at him from behind, clasping one hand round his mouth to silence him, and with the other drive the knife-blade into his kidneys, or simply cut his throat. Combined with the practical aspect of this type of fighting was the mental approach to it. Looking back now it seems incredible that during those spring days and evenings, and set against the quiet, peaceful background of that lovely old house, we schooled ourselves into a state of ferocious intent, which no wild animal could outdo as he sprang upon his prey.

This type of warfare hardly went hand-in-hand with traditional army discipline. With us there was no question of superiority in rank, we all knew each other by our first names; and though we trained ourselves to work individually, at the same time we developed a terrific team-spirit among us. When we went on an exercise, each could sense what the other chap was going to do, how he would react to any crisis which might arise.

Appleyard himself was typical of the spirit which animated all our efforts. He had been a champion skier, ski-ing for Cambridge University. Just before the war he had won the famous Roberts of Kandahar ski-race in a blinding snowstorm in Norway, beating the Norwegians on their own ground. He was much more at home in a pair of old slacks and his ski-ing pullover than in his army uniform. Paradoxically, although he was enthusiastic in his cold-blooded schemes for dealing with the enemy, he was deeply religious. It was as if to him the Nazis represented the Devil himself, who must be wiped out at whatever the cost, and in the most expedient fashion. He felt that he was fighting the good fight.

It was this religious fervour, together with his spell-binding charms, which won Appleyard the devotion of everyone who worked with him, and the respect of Combined Operations, to whom we owed help and encouragement at the beginning. The Army had no time for us, in fact they were against the whole idea of this type of fighting. It was not until much later, when the Commandos had proved themselves one hundred per cent successful, that the War Office realized that we had got something.

Even now March-Phillips was spending a lot of time in London unravelling some of the red-tape with which the Army were trying to tie us up from going into action with our plans.

So, we were all tremendously thrilled when March-Phillips came back from London with permission from everyone concerned for us to set about our job. The Navy were playing along with us to the extent of giving us an old torpedo-boat, complete with crew, which would get us across the Channel to the French coast. We had a Lieutenant Van of the Belgium Navy to help us in navigation and to teach us to work with the boat crew during landing and re-embarking.

Van was a volatile, adventurous type, who had already carried out numerous single-handed raids into Occupied Europe. At the time of the fall of France one of his most important assignments had been to collect General de Gaulle's wife and daughter, in hiding in a village on the Brittany coast, and get them to England. It was planned that the General's wife and daughter would be waiting in a small boat off shore.

When Van arrived at the rendezvous, however, no one was there. He knew that the vicinity was occupied by the Germans, but although he was wearing a British Naval officer's uniform, he decided to go ashore in order to find out what had happened. His boldness succeeded, he was not challenged by anyone. But his feelings can be imagined when he learned from agents in the village that de Gaulle's wife had left with her daughter by air the day before for South America. No one had troubled to let Van know that his dangerous journey was unnecessary.

The old torpedo-boat was very small, so that we could carry only a light machine-gun by way of armament. This would not be much good against the fast, heavily-armed German E-boats which ranged the Channel. We could not even carry a torpedo, since we had put a dinghy where it was supposed to be. It was in the dinghy that we would slip ashore from the torpedo-boat. We had discovered that rowing made too much noise with the splash of water from the oars, so we used paddles, each man putting his paddle into the water at the same time and not taking it out, but twisting the blade-edge against the water for the forward-stroke, Red Indian fashion.

Our first raid was to be directed against a German military post near Cherbourg. One morning Appleyard and March-Phillips called us all into a conference to plan the operation. Our preparations were aided by a scale-model reproduction of the area we were to raid, which had been made from information supplied by agents. Our object was to take the post by surprise, and bring back prisoners for information. We would go as soon as the weather and the tide permitted, which would not be for several days. Since surprise was vital to our success, our intentions had to be one hundred per cent secret. In order to maintain security, we went off on mock expeditions nearly every night for a week or so. We left Poole in our torpedo-boat at night and returned in the early hours, to convey the impression to anyone interested who might have been observing us that we were still in training.

Then one night we left Poole in pitch darkness with tide and weather perfect for our enterprise.

This was the real thing.

Chapter 7

# The Casquets
# Lighthouse

Besides the machine-gun our only armaments were two
hand grenades, a Sten gun and a revolver to each man. Not
much to go to war with, alone. There was not much space
aboard the torpedo-boat, so most of us sat in the dinghy, out of
the crew's way.

The sea slid past us, black and reflecting the stars in the sky.
We talked very little, and when we did only in whispers. My
thoughts, like those of the others, were concentrated on the task
ahead. A watchful eye was kept for signs of enemy craft, but we
encountered none.

About a mile from the shore, where we estimated the Nazi post
to be, the torpedo-boat's engines cut out and we drifted silently
forward; the only sound was the sea lapping against the vessel's
sides. Quickly we lowered the dinghy – the need for silence was
stronger than ever before, we were dangerously near the enemy;
and so not a word was said as we took our pre-arranged places.

March-Phillips was in the bows to direct us, as we paddled
for the rocky shore in the darkness ahead. Unfortunately, he had
made a miscalculation; he was using a land compass to steer us
by, instead of a sea compass. The two compasses work very dif-
ferently, and as a result we found that we were a long way off our
course. We had left the dinghy with two of the party to wait for
us by some rocks while we waded ashore. Instead of being faced
by a relatively small military post, we were slap-bang in front of
a Nazi marine-battery. We knew what it was from information we
had received before setting out, the place was manned by some
three hundred marines. And there were only ten of us.

As we crouched on the beach we could clearly see the sentries
mounting guard all along the barbed-wire between them and us.
Obviously, we could not attack against such a large force with any
hope of success, yet it was in all our minds that to return without having achieved some results was mortifying. "I'm damned
if we're coming all this way for nothing," Appleyard whispered.

"Let's have a go at the sentries," March-Phillips whispered in reply. "If we pick a couple each for some hand-grenade practice, we're bound to do a bit of damage."

We spread ourselves along the beach before the barbed-wire, and selected a couple of sentries apiece, as, all unsuspecting, they stood there, or paced up and down. March-Phillips carried a hunting horn, which he would blow as a signal whenever it was a question of every man for himself. Now we were to take the first note of his horn as a signal to throw our grenades, and then dash for the dinghy.

March-Phillips' hunting horn sounded suddenly loud and clear, and its musical note had barely died away before all hell was let loose, as twenty grenades exploded almost in unison. The two sentries I had aimed my grenade at seemed to disappear in the burst and flash of explosive. Immediately the whole place was a blaze of searchlights, raking the sky and the beaches. By now each of us was heading for the water's edge, which remained in the shadows, out of range of the probing fingers of light.

The Nazis were completely taken by surprise, and it was a few moments before they let fly with their machine-guns. Then every machine-gun in the place must have started firing, the row was so terrific. But as we scrambled back into the dinghy, we could congratulate ourselves that they must be firing at each other; not a single shot came in our direction. All of us safe, we paddled off into the darkness, looking back to see what damage we had done. In the illumination of the searchlights, figures were dashing all over the place. The machine-guns were still going strong, and we saw an ambulance car driving off.

But now we were preoccupied with our own troubles. In the pitch darkness it was impossible for us to make out the torpedo-boat, waiting somewhere out to sea for our return. Rather belatedly we realized that while we had practised paddling away from her in darkness, we had omitted to practise finding her again.

Lieutenant Van, who was in command of the torpedo-boat, and his crew could see us against the lights of the shore, paddling around, hopelessly lost. They tried to hail us, but failed to make themselves heard. Nearly an hour we floundered about, the danger to us growing every minute, for daylight was approaching, and we should easily be seen by the Germans on the shore. That would be the finish for us.

There was only one thing that could save us, and Van did it. He switched on all the lights of the torpedo-boat, giving us his position, and we headed straight for it. But he had revealed his presence to the Nazis, and at once every gun in the battery opened up. The battery had not got us in range, and Van quickly put his lights out again, but as we scrambled aboard, leaving the dinghy behind, shells from the battery were falling all around. And now the searchlights were directed upon us, as the torpedo-boat's engines gathered speed, and we headed into the protective darkness. Luck and the bad aim of the Nazi gunners were with us, and we zigzagged out of danger for home.

Exhausted but happy, we all relaxed and discussed our night's work. We had failed to achieve what we had set out to do, which was to bring back prisoners for information purposes, but we calculated that we had put a score or more Nazis out of action, without loss to ourselves. We had also learned valuable lessons, to put into practice on our next little trip. Above all, we had struck a daring blow against the enemy, and got away with it. That was what filled me with exhilaration. I had been in action against the Nazis. I had, I felt confident, accounted for at least two of those sentries. At last I had received my baptism under fire.

We were back at Poole in the grey light of the morning, dog-tired and half asleep, but happy and immensely proud of ourselves. A lorry took us back through the tree-lined Dorset roads and lanes, fresh and clear in the early light. It seemed difficult to believe that but a short while ago we had been letting loose death and destruction on a French beach, eighty miles away.

Back at the old house I fell into my bed, utterly exhausted. I prayed to God, thanking Him for giving me His protection; and if at the back of my mind, I retained a picture of two figures disintegrating in the blinding flash and explosion of my grenades, the picture faded as I fell asleep.

We were given a fortnight's leave in which to recover from the effects of our adventure, to relax and refresh ourselves in readiness for the next job. My father and mother had left their relatives' home in Barry to make a home for themselves at Isleworth, outside London. I spent my leave with them, and thought they showed a not unnatural curiosity about my contribution to the war effort. I was able to satisfy them that I was still an interpreter attached to the War Office. So, they remained in blissful ignorance of my real job, and their fears that I was likely to be involved in any danger were lulled.

During my leave I met de G. in London two or three times. He introduced me to his girl-friend, who was French, and she, in turn, introduced me to another French girl, a friend of hers. She was named Lucette, and I found her very attractive. It was not until I had spent a lot of time with her that I understood what she was. De G. had taken it for granted that I was aware of the profession of his girl-friend and Lucette.

The two girls shared a flat off Bond Street. It was very nicely furnished, and a prim little maidservant used to look after them. The flat always smelled of the loveliest perfume. There was always plenty of young chaps there, dropping in for drinks, and it seemed to me to be very gay, the radio or a gramophone always playing. I used to see Lucette in the afternoon usually, and we would lie together in the scented gloom, talking about France, and how we looked forward to going back there after the war.

One reason why I was so naïve about Lucette was that she never asked me for money, and I had always been told that the most important thing was not the lover, but his cash. Lucette was full of gaiety, with the fresh bloom of youth upon her pretty face, and her body was white and soft in my arms, and I was a young innocent.

It was back to Blandford for de G. and me, already the old house was humming with preparations for another raid against the Nazis. This time our objective was to be the *Casquets* Lighthouse on the Channel Islands, which had been grabbed by the Nazis two years before. Our orders were to capture the crew of about half a dozen German naval types who manned the lighthouse, operated the wireless and kept guard. We were to bring them back to England and put the wireless installation out of action, but the light itself was to be left unharmed, since it provided a guide for British bombers and help to Allied shipping in the area.

We left on the night of 2 September 1942, planning to reach our objective by about midnight. Once again, the sea was calm and there was no moon; we took the same course as on our previous trip, this time using a sea-compass, however. We had learned that a land-compass was no good, even on a short distance; and also, that we must devise a method of finding our torpedo-boat again in the darkness, once we had left her in the dinghy. First, we tried keeping in touch by means of a rope attached to the torpedo-boat, but it would get caught by weeds and rocks. We tried a field-telephone, but that also was unsatisfactory. At last we found the perfect way: a light on board which, while it was invisible to the naked eye, could be seen by us using a special instrument.

It was shortly before midnight when the torpedo-boat stood off from the little rock island on which the lighthouse was built, and we paddled towards it in the dinghy. Above us the great blazing eye flashed its brilliant beam into the darkness. Our dinghy scraped against the rocks, and then we were scrambling our way through the barbed-wire which barred our path briefly.

Led by Appleyard and March-Phillips we arrived at the light-house entrance, to find the door unlocked. In we went, to find a Nazi naval officer busy in his office over some official papers. When he saw us, with our blackened faces and our Colt revolvers in our hands, it was quite obvious that he thought he must be experiencing a nightmare. As we moved forward to grab him he just passed out in sheer fright. We had to slap his face vigorously to bring him round.

Upstairs in the sleeping-quarters we came upon the rest of the lighthouse-crew, fast asleep. Six of them, and they were so petri-fied by our appearance that they put up no resistance. One or two of them were wearing hair-nets in bed, so that at first, we thought they were girls. They seemed to be very young and utterly terri-fied. While some of us hustled our prisoners down to the waiting dinghy, the rest of us set about smashing up the radio installa-tion and removing what armaments there were and throwing them into the sea. We also took with us two or three Nazi flags as souvenirs.

Our dinghy was supposed to hold only twelve, so that with the seven Nazis it was a bit of a tight squeeze, and the boat lay very low in the water. However, we paddled back to the torpe-do-boat as best we could. The poor devils turned out to be pretty bad sailors, for on our way back we ran into a heavy swell, which made them all sea-sick.

On our return I was present while one of the prisoners was interrogated by Army Intelligence officers, whose methods seemed to me to be admirably simple. The Nazi revealed that he was married with two children, and was asked: "And no doubt you want to see your wife and children again? You do? Then tell us everything you know, if you don't, we'll chuck you in the sea and you can swim back to your wife and kids."

After this raid we went straight down to Falmouth in Devon to learn how to use a new type of landing craft. Then back to Dorset and some training in newer types of guns and smaller weapons. We learnt how to shoot at night, by painting the sights of our revolvers with luminous paint. We also picked up some tips on street-fighting. Then off on our next job, which was a raid on Cherbourg.

This time our objective was to take only a few prisoners for interrogation purposes. The part of the Cherbourg coast at which we arrived was very rocky, and to reach the Nazi military post we had selected we had to scale the cliffs. That achieved we found we had picked quite the wrong time for our call. Instead of a mere dozen Germans as anticipated, we had arrived at the same time as the relief-guard, and we were faced by about three dozen Nazis. There were twelve of us. We were determined to grab some prisoners, so rushed the position, firing everything we had, in an effort to overcome any opposition by surprise.

I fired my Sten gun point-blank at one chap who flung himself at me, and in the flash and glare I saw him disintegrate in a mess of blood and shattered bones and flesh. Then we had to turn and run for it, with the Germans hot on our heels. Appleyard slipped on the rocks and hurt his foot, but we got away all right. If we had failed to bag some prisoners, we had at least managed to kill a few Nazis.

It was not until later, when we were heading back home, that I realized that I had shot another human being to bits before my eyes. In the heat of the fight, automaton-like, I had been firing my Sten gun; I had not thought about it. Now, as my mind turned to my father and mother, and how worried they would be if they knew what I was really up to, I thought involuntarily of that dead Nazi's parents. What would they be thinking when they learned of their son's death, their son whom I had killed?

My sombre reflections were interrupted by the alarm being raised-two German E-boats were suddenly spotted, heading in our direction. Not only were they more powerfully armed than us, they also possessed superior speed. Lieutenant Van's only way of escape was to take a chance and cross one of our own minefields. The two E-boats stood off, waiting to see us blown to pieces. But they were to be disappointed, either because of Van's navigation skill, or our relatively shallow draught, or just sheer luck, we managed to get through. In all the excitement, while I waited tensed with my scalp crawling, for our boat and all of us with it to be blown sky-high, my thoughts about the Nazi I had killed were pushed aside.

By now the War Office top brass were beginning to catch on that this idea of Appleyard's and March-Phillips' was worthwhile developing, and we became increasingly busy, making reconnaissance raids all along the French coast, to pick up every scrap of information against the day when the Allies would return to France.

I started work with a Major Y. and two others, called Paddy and Fitchell, on a plan which had a Luftwaffe airfield on the Brittany coast as our objective. Major Y. was trained in intelligence work and had come from the Royal Artillery. He had been a lawyer before the war, and struck me as possessing a cold-blooded nature and a consuming hatred of the Nazis.

We aimed to arrive one night and sabotage as many enemy fighter planes as we could in the time at our disposal. The idea was to land in the vicinity by parachute, and then after the operation had been completed hide by the seashore to be picked up by a submarine. Major Y. had carried out some parachute-jumps, but neither Paddy nor Fitchell had done any, so I took them up to Ringway to put them through the hoop. I was looking forward to the thrill of jumping again, and imbued the others with my own anticipation and enthusiasm.

Paddy and Fitchell were very fit anyway, and took to the initial training at Ringway fast and without any qualms. On the morning when they were all set for their first jump, and the three of us were waiting for our plane – I was to jump with them, going first – we saw another aircraft circling the airfield, and then a pair of figures jump from it, one after the other. They were, we learned afterwards, two high-ranking officers from the War Office, who had come up to Ringway to study parachute-jumping at first-hand.

"There you are," I said to Paddy and Fitchell, "see how easy it is."

We stood and watched, Paddy and Fitchell with their faces tense, their mouths slightly open. I was smiling and wishing impatiently I was up there already. And then as the two men jumped and began falling my heart seemed to stop beating. Their parachutes did not open. Down and down the pair of figures plunged. Down and down, and their parachutes never opening. Fitchell turned away just before they hit the ground, and I could hear him behind me vomit.

It never occurred to me that my two pupils and myself should postpone our jumps. A few minutes later the three of us got into the plane that was taking us up, and presently I was plunging downwards myself. I felt the old familiar tug at my harness, and the 'chute opened above me and I heard the wind humming through the cords overhead, and that indescribable exhilaration flooded my entire being. I glanced up at the two other 'chutes which had blossomed out one after the other against the grey-blue sky.

Paddy and Fitchell had followed me all right, they had made their first jump.

# Chapter 8

# Cherbourg and a Luftwaffe Airfield In Brittany

A fter the Ringway course was through, Paddy and Fitchell, both of whom had proved themselves first-class parachute-jumpers, and I, turned up at a secret school which had been started at a house in the Thames Valley, known as School K. It specialized in instructing agents in the use of types of explosives for sabotage purposes.

Y. was already there when we arrived, and had arranged for the fuselage of a shot-down Luftwaffe fighter to be set up in the grounds of the house, so that we could familiarize ourselves with its structure. This new explosive was dangerous to handle – once the safety device was removed the bomb was extremely sensitive, the slightest touch would explode it – and it was essential that we should discover exactly how and where to place the explosive so as to cause the maximum damage to the plane with the minimum of risk to ourselves. We had to learn all this under night-time conditions.

Our training took six weeks, during which we carried out mock raids on a number of our own airfields, each time with complete success, even though the airfield selected received warnings of our attempt upon it. We returned to Blandford to wait for favourable weather. Appleyard and March-Phillips were getting ready for another raid in the Cherbourg area, but this time they were trying a new kind of landing-boat made of canvas and which was collapsible. Appleyard had broken his ankle during the raid on the *Casquets* Lighthouse, and could not go ashore with the others, but was to accompany them in the torpedo-boat, which he could command and wait off-shore, while the little canvas boat went in. Y. and I learned that the weather would not be favourable for a parachute-drop, so it was decided that we would go on our operation by a fishing-boat; the submarine would rendezvous as already arranged to pick us up.

On 12 September 1942, the same night that we set off, Appleyard and March-Phillips, de G. and Hayes and the rest of them also left, they as were going to Portsmouth by lorry. We were all very gay, waving each other good-bye, not thinking that for some it was the last hours of their lives. We were all singing and joking as we left for our different destinations and destinies. We were heading for Falmouth, and we drove through the night to arrive there early next day, and went aboard the fishing-boat, to await calmer weather. The sea was impossibly rough, even for our sturdy little vessel. Listening to the radio in the evening, we heard that a raiding-party on the Cherbourg coast had been wiped out by the Nazis, all had been killed or taken prisoner. We were stunned by this news, but we had to try to put it out of our minds and think only of our job ahead of us.

Our fishing-boat had once belonged to a Breton fisherman, who had come over to Cornwall, saying that he had escaped from France. It was later discovered that he was a German agent, and his boat had been taken over by our Intelligence. It was proving very useful for carrying British agents over to the French coast, as it was exactly like every other Breton fishing-vessel which the Germans allowed in French fishing-waters. The crew were Royal Navy types, with a young naval officer in command.

The sea continued impossibly rough, and the days passed one by one while we waited impatiently for the word to go. Times like that are the worst, for there is nothing to do but just wait and wait. Then at last the word came. There was still a gale blowing, but according to the reports it should be all right for us by the time we reached the French coast.

Everything went well until we were off Land's End, then it was so rough that the boat seemed to be standing right up on end. Even the crew were sea-sick, it was horrible. I have never been sea-sick in my life, but then I wished I had been able to be sick; I really felt ill and my stomach was in my mouth. It was so bad that the anti-aircraft gun we had on board started to fire by itself, and one of our naval torpedo-boats in the vicinity thought that we were firing at them, so they came to board us. We managed to explain who we were, and they let us go on our way.

There was no sign of the weather getting better. When in the early hours of the next morning we reached the French coast, it was just as bad, but we decided to launch our little dinghy and try the landing after all, while it was still dark.

Major Y. said he would go first with Paddy, two of the crew would row them ashore and then come back for Fitchell and me. We managed to lower the dinghy and with difficulty to get Major

Y. and Paddy and the two sailors into her. But it was hopeless, the dinghy would never make it, the gale was blowing harder, the seas growing more mountainous.

Now the dinghy tried to make back for the fishing-boat, and we were striving to get near it, but, in the darkness, we just got farther apart. We kept throwing a rope to the dinghy, but for a long time no one in her managed to get hold of it. At last the rope was grabbed and we got the four chaps on board again. Our attempt had to be abandoned, and feeling dejected and frustrated we set course for home.

Back at Blandford we found Appleyard, the only one to return from that disastrous Cherbourg raid. He told us how he and March-Phillips (who had been married only a few weeks before) and the others had crept in pitch darkness into the little bay, which was their objective, on their silent auxiliary engine. March-Phillips and the rest got into the canvas boat, leaving Appleyard in the torpedo-boat off-shore.

March-Phillips and his crowd landed and set off for the Nazi military post a short distance inland. They found it to be more heavily guarded than they had anticipated, so March-Phillips decided to do nothing about it then, but that it would be a good idea to return later with a larger raiding-party and attack the post. He and his party had almost got back to the beach and their canvas boat when they heard a small Nazi patrol approaching. March-Phillips wanted a prisoner or two to show something for his night's trip. The patrol walked straight into the ambush, but the Nazis put up such a fight that all seven of them were killed.

March-Phillips was searching the bodies for maps and other documents, when another and much larger patrol arrived out of the darkness, attracted by the sound of firing. To attempt to fight this lot would have been suicidal, so March-Phillips led the way to the beach. Everyone fell into the boat and had got about a hundred yards out when the Nazis sent up a flare. Immediately a hail of fire was turned upon the little canvas boat.

Appleyard heard the shooting and saw gun-flashes against the dark sky; then he heard March-Phillips' voice, calling across the water: "Getaway ... getaway." He realized it was meant for him and the torpedo-boat, but he waited; he still might be able to do something to help the others. By now March-Phillips and three of his comrades had been killed, and the rest, some of them wounded, were flung into the water as the boat sank.

Appleyard was unable to get his vessel close into the shore because of the shallow water, and he could see no definite target at which to return the fire. He brought the torpedo-boat in as close as possible and cruised around the bay, calling by whistle and showing a signal light, hoping to pick someone up. He was under constant gunfire from the shore, and one of his boat's engines was hit and put out of action. With the approach of daybreak, he had no option but to make straight back for home, taking a direct course through the minefields, without mishap. He was escorted into Portsmouth by Spitfires sent out to ward off any enemy air-attack.

De G. was one of those who had been wounded and captured on this job, and I later learned was badly knocked about by the Gestapo; but he came through it all in the end, alive and kicking. The only one of March-Phillips' party to escape was Hayes. He was a very strong swimmer, and managed to swim away from the scene quite a distance without being spotted. He got ashore and a friendly farmer helped him to reach Paris, where he contacted one of our secret agents. Pretending to be deaf and dumb, he used to go to football matches and cinemas. Then Hayes decided to get back to England and got over the border into Spain, but here his good luck ended. The Spanish police nabbed him and handed him over to the Gestapo, who imprisoned him in the notorious Fresnes prison in Paris, where he was later shot.

Of course, I did not learn all this at the time. In fact, I was told that Hayes story later when I was a prisoner-of-war in the infamous Stalag Luft III of 'Wooden Horse' fame. One of my fellow prisoners there had previously been in Fresnes in a cell next to that occupied by Hayes.

Appleyard was in a very bad state as a result of the Cherbourg raid disaster, and we all felt that the bottom had fallen out of our world. I threw myself even more energetically into making plans with Major Y., Paddy and Fitchell, for another go at that Nazi airfield in Brittany.

It was decided that instead of being picked up by a submarine we should, after having completed the job, make our way through France to Marseilles, and then by boat to Lisbon, from where we would be flown back to London. This time, too, we would make the trip across to Brittany by torpedo-boat. By now Appleyard was worried that security regarding our work had loosened. The local people had read in the newspapers, or heard over the radio, all about the Cherbourg business, and they could not help noticing the absence of March-Phillips and those who had accompanied him; and they were soon putting two and two together. So there should be no danger that any inkling of our raid on the airfield should leak out, we all travelled in an ordinary army convoy to Torquay, to give the impression we were going on manoeuvres.

The torpedo-boat was awaiting us in the little harbour at Torquay and, as was our usual plan, we put out to sea in the darkness just before midnight.

We reached the Brittany coast in the early hours of the morning. Everything went according to plan. Y., Paddy, Fitchell and I said good-bye to Appleyard, got into the dinghy and we were rowed ashore by two of the torpedo-boat's crew. While the dinghy returned to the torpedo-boat, the four of us made for a small wood not very far from the airfield. There we would spend the day, then carry out the job when night fell again. We made ourselves at home deep in some bushes, with one of us taking it in turn as sentry. We got some sleep – we wanted to be fresh for the night's work. In the afternoon we went out to reconnoitre, getting as near the airfield as we could. It was surrounded by barbed-wire, and having decided which was the best spot to cut the wire, we returned to our hiding-place.

Nightfall, and the hour for action.

As we approached the airfield everything was silent. On our bellies, the four of us reached the barbed-wire. Then Fitchell and I edged forward; while I held the wire Fitchell worked away with the wire-cutters. When he had made a big enough gap, I put down a handkerchief to mark the place, so that when the time came for us to get out we would know exactly where it was, without having to look for it and lose time.

We divided into two pairs, Y. and Paddy, and Fitchell and I, and wishing each other luck slipped through the wire. We carried enough explosive between us to blow up twelve planes, so while Y. and Paddy took one part of the airfield, Fitchell and I took another. With a sixpenny-bit I unscrewed the inspection-plate over the engine of our first plane, inserted the explosive in the shape of a magnetic limpet bomb, took out the pin, and carefully replaced the inspection-plate, screwing it down again.

Thanks to our practice on the shot-down Luftwaffe fighter-plane fuselage, we knew exactly where to find what we wanted in the darkness. But it was a nerve-racking business. Once the pin had been removed from the bomb the slightest vibration would set it off and we would blow up with it. The object of the explosive was that it should go off when the pilot started the engine, thus destroying himself with the aircraft. We were working amidst the Nazis, a pilot or guard might appear at any moment and catch us, and although a cool breeze was blowing across the airfield, the perspiration was running down my face.

At last Fitchell and I completed our deadly work with six of the planes, and now we had to get away as fast as possible; we reached the cement runway which had to be crossed to get back to where the white handkerchief marked the gap in the barbed-wire. I sent Fitchell first. Then, when I was about half-way across the runway, all the searchlights around the airfield suddenly went on. I dived into the shadows, then wriggled my way into the first hiding-place I could find, and found myself in a latrine.

While I was wondering how long I would have to stay there, a shadowy figure came in, so I acted as though I was passing water. The man saw me in the semi-darkness and said something in German and laughed. I guessed he could not really see me, so I risked it and replied: "*Ya, ya.*" The other laughed still more, so I decided I must have made the appropriate reply, and he went away, still laughing.

I waited about ten minutes, but nobody else came in, then all the lights outside died out. I slipped out and soon found the white handkerchief. When I got to our hide-out in the woods, the three others were already there; they thought that I had been caught. Y. and Paddy had planted their explosives all right, and we could congratulate ourselves that we had accomplished our mission.

We enjoyed one good joke between us before we separated, Y. and Paddy pairing off, and Fitchell accompanying me, to start the long journey to the other side of France. I mentioned to Paddy the incident of the German coming into the latrine while I was hiding there, and Paddy let out an exclamation.

"Something like that happened to me," he said. "I got caught in the airfield lights the same as you. And I dodged into what turned out to be a latrine, and found someone in there. I decided to bluff it out, and said one of the few bits of German I know, a Shakespeare quotation: 'For this relief, much thanks.' And I laughed, and the other chap laughed too, and said: '*Ya, ya*'."

It was then that we realized that in the darkness of that latrine Paddy and I had mistaken each other for Nazis.

So, we parted, each of us going our own way, wishing each other luck, and looking forward to when we would meet again. I went off into the night with Fitchell. Now that we had disposed of the explosives we felt much lighter as we walked - they had been quite a weight to carry - and also now that our mission had been achieved, we felt as if a weight had been taken off our stomachs. For food we had not much, only concentrated stuff, we as were hoping to feed off the land as we went; in France at that time of the year there are at any rate always plenty of apples on the trees.

We had been on our way for an hour when we heard a dull explosion behind us, and we knew that the first of those Luftwaffe planes had been blown to bits. We waited a little and then came more explosions from the same direction, and we grinned at each other in the darkness. We pushed on, to get as far away from the airfield as we could during that night. We had to go very carefully, skirting villages by going through fields. We had got used to the darkness and were able to see our way quite well. Not being able to speak – in the night voices carry far – we were left each with our own thoughts.

Walking by night and sleeping by day we travelled on. It was really ideal weather, beautiful autumn sunshine during the day and the nights were mild. For food we managed all right; we could not cook anything, we were afraid to light a fire, but we obtained fruit and raw vegetables and our concentrated foods kept us going. Being in army uniform, we could never afford to be seen by any civilian, since we did not know who was for and who was against us.

And so, without untoward incident or mishap we reached unoccupied France, crossing the demarcation line near Poitiers. Now we buried the arms we had been carrying, and put on workman's overalls, which we had brought with us specially, over our uniforms, so that if we were caught we would still be treated as soldiers, and not handed over by the Vichy authorities to the Germans as spies or saboteurs. As soldiers the only thing that could happen to us if we were caught was that we should be interned. Fitchell spoke no French, so I did all the talking.

From now on we fed well and slept comfortably, all the way to Marseilles we had the addresses of agents and members of the underground ready to help us. We could travel much more quickly than foot-slogging it by night as we had been doing. We got lifts by lorries, cars, and horse-wagons, and we borrowed bicycles. Even so, the entire journey from Brittany to Marseilles took us six weeks; sometimes it was necessary to lie low for two or three days on account of the danger from Vichy police or members of the Gestapo at points on our way; and we always had to watch out for German or Italian troops who were moving about the countryside. Despite these hazards I enjoyed the trip enormously; it was wonderful to be back in France, and speaking the language I loved again.

Fitchell and I arrived at the outskirts of Marseilles, still in our workmen's overalls worn over our uniform, on the back of a farmer's wagon. Our first job was to pick up our contact in Marseilles whom, we were instructed, we should find at the buffet de la gare. And so, we proceeded to the railway station and found the buffet crowded with German and Italian soldiers and sailors, together with French civilians, a motley collection of Arabs and other dark-skinned types, and plenty of women, some of them obviously prostitutes.

At first Fitchell and I felt a little nervous at the prospect of having to barge in amongst such a formidable array of enemy in uniform. Then I recalled a story about the refreshment room at Charing Cross Station in London, which was always thronged with Allied servicemen. Two British officers had dressed themselves up in German army officers' uniforms and marched into the refreshment room, ordered sandwiches and tea in assumed guttural accents. Despite their appearance, they remained there for over an hour, filling themselves with tea, sandwiches and cakes and behaving as conspicuously as they could, without anyone taking the slightest notice of them. There was certainly nothing suspicious about Fitchell's appearance and mine. We both looked like a couple of workmen, and so, confident that we would get away with it, we went into the buffet.

Nobody took any notice of us as we pushed our way through the closely packed throng, hearing several languages being spoken on all sides, to order something to eat and drink. We reached the counter and gave our order, and I was wondering how long we should have to wait before we met our contact, when I heard a woman's voice in my ear. I turned round and stared into the heavily made-up face of a blonde, whose profession was unmistakable. Fitchell grinned self-consciously at her inviting glances as she spoke to us endearingly in French. I was about to turn away from her to show that we were not interested, when I caught the words: "Le Chabanais."

I turned back to her with fresh interest, at the same time giving Fitchell a significant nudge. He too stared hard at the blonde. In a few moments the three of us were pushing our way, arm-in-arm, out of the buffet, followed by knowing looks and winks from the onlookers around us. Outside the station we got into a rickety old taxi and the girl directed the driver to an address in the street called Le Chabanais, which lay in the old part of Marseilles by the waterfront.

Marseilles was strongly pro-British, and consequently was a hotbed of Allied espionage and Axis counter-espionage. Streets like Le Chabanais, snaking through the vast water-front district and criss-crossed with tortuous alleys and culs-de-sac, crammed with crumbling old houses and tenements, dotted with cafés, brothels and other places of dubious amusement, provided numerous hide-outs for our agents. The house to which the blonde took Fitchell and me was in fact a brothel. It was late evening – Fitchell and I had purposely arrived at Marseilles as it was growing dark – and now the shadows were falling; soon the city would lie under the blanket of the black-out.

Fitchell and I followed the girl into the front of the house, which was furnished with tables at which sat soldiers and sailors, Nazis and Italians – and I noticed two Japanese officers – with here and there men in civilian clothes. Drinking and smoking with some of the customers were the girls of the house. But most of them were parading round to the rather tinny music from a gramophone. Even as we stood there, accustoming our eyes to the garish lighting, the haze of cigarette smoke, and our ears to the music, the chatter and laughter, a soldier beckoned to one of the parading girls who had taken his fancy, and after a few words together he followed her out of the room through some beaded curtains, upstairs.

The blonde led us to a corner table, and called across to a dark fat woman in a black dress who was serving drinks. While drinks were being brought us, the blonde told me quietly, with one arm lovingly round my neck, as if I was a prospective client, that one of the girls would ogle me, and I was to pretend to choose her and duly accompany her upstairs. Fitchell was to remain with the blonde, who would take him upstairs.

Soon after we had been served with our drinks, a gipsy-faced girl passed by, her huge dark eyes laughing at me. I smiled back at her, and she pranced over to me at once, showering me with endearments and throwing herself on to my knee. I went hot all over as her olive-skinned arms entwined round my neck and my hands clasped her thighs.

However, I managed to act as if I was suitably attracted to her, and she took both my hands in hers and led me from the table. Then she placed one arm round her waist and the other over her breasts and nibbled my ear. "Look as if you like it," she whispered, "and are going to like it even more." And she pushed me through the beaded curtains, and we were ascending the dark stairs. I could hear feminine laughter and a man's guffaw as I followed the gipsy girl along a dimly-lit passage, then up another flight of stairs, until halfway along another passage she opened a door, switched on the light inside, and I went into the room.

The girl closed the door after me. The room was barely furnished. A bed, chair, dressing-table and wash-basin with two or three towels hung on it, and a large bottle of disinfectant. The girl moved to a cupboard and, giving me a strangely demure look, took out a dressing-robe and wrapped it round her. "You had better take your clothes off," she said, "just in case the Gestapo poke their dirty noses in here."

And so, while she took my uniform and hid it at the back of the cupboard, leaving my overalls and shirt on the chair with my underclothes, she talked to me quietly, explaining that she was my contact in Marseilles. I was to stay in her room, to await orders from London about getting away to Lisbon. The girl who had met us at the railway station was Fitchell's contact, and she would shelter him in her room until orders came for him; how and when he should get away. From now on Fitchell and I were to act separately, rely entirely on our contacts to tell us what to do.

Both the blonde and the gipsy girl were prostitutes, but also worked as agents for the owner of the brothel, a Frenchman, who was himself an Allied secret agent. He had taken over the house in Le Chabanais before the war, as a cover for his activities, and employed several other girls in the house as agents. Besides helping people like ourselves, by the nature of their profession they picked up all sorts of information useful to the Allies from their customers. I spent most of my time in the gipsy girl's room, sleeping in her bed, while she entertained her clients in another room. On one or two occasions Fitchell and I ventured together as far as another French agent's place, known as the Café de la Joliette, down on the waterfront. There we could get a whiff of the sea and a sight of the shipping of all kinds that crowded the harbour. But it was dangerous to leave the brothel too often; the Gestapo and Vichy police were constantly on the prowl.

The brothel was a Moorish-type house, and the window of the room I was occupying opened on to a flat roof. Late one night the gipsy girl slipped in to warn me that the Gestapo were raiding the neighbourhood, carrying out their house-to-house searches. I was getting my clothes on fast, when suddenly the door opened. The girl and I whipped round to face a man in the doorway. He was in civilian clothes, with Gestapo stamped all over him.

As he started to say something in French, with a thick German accent, I jumped at him. I had got my shoes on, and I caught him a terrific kick in his groin. He doubled up with a grunt of agony, and I brought the edge of my right hand with all my force against the side of the neck below the ear. He fell flat on his face. The blow should have killed him; it was meant to, but I was not sure that I had hit him in the exact fatal spot. So, as he lay there I crashed my shoe-heel against his temple. I felt the thin bone crunch, and knew for certain I had put paid to him.

The girl was telling me that he was probably a Gestapo agent, who had been in the front of the house, and had followed her upstairs, when she had come up to warn me. She helped me get the body out of the window on to the flat roof. I went out after it. I could see the reflection above me of the huge spotlights which the Gestapo had brought on lorries and cars, and which lit up the entire street. I pushed the dead man over the side of the roof. I landed beside him about fifteen feet below in a cul-de-sac. I dragged the corpse through a window into a passage. Along the passage, down some stone steps to a cellar. Through a door and up more stone steps. Finally, still hanging on to the dead Gestapo agent, I landed up in the basement of a tumble-down tenement house, several hundred yards distant from Le Chabanais.

Here I was taken care of by a married couple, the parents of the agent who ran the Café de la Joliette. As a matter of fact, they hid the dead man under some stairs; later he would be thrown into the harbour. Then, when the danger was over, I made my way back to Le Chabanais and the gipsy girl's room. Fitchell had also been hidden away, and so we could breathe more freely again. I had been there five days when my contact told me I was leaving that night.

A few hours after nightfall I was guided down to the water-front and slipped aboard a fishing vessel. I knew it was a boat used by our agents to bring arms, guns, explosives and medical supplies from Gibraltar to Marseilles, to be distributed to the Maquis. But to my delighted surprise the first man to meet me as I came on board was Emile. We had a great celebration as we slipped out of the harbour, bound for Lisbon.

Emile was still as boastful and warm-hearted as ever, and enjoying himself hugely in his new job. He had already made several of these trips, landing the stuff under the very noses of the enemy. I knew it must be a terribly risky job; the Gestapo and the Vichy police were very much aware of what was going on and used the most ruthless measures against these activities. Emile was, of course, full of his hair's-breadth escapes and the exciting means by which he eluded his enemies. He certainly seemed to bear a charmed life, and was, in fact, never caught throughout the whole of the war.

Four uneventful days of calm weather and then our little fishing-boat lay off Lisbon harbour. A small motor-boat came out and took me off, after my grateful adieux to Emile and the crew. Unobtrusively I was put ashore, a waiting car took me to an hotel, where I was allowed time for a bath and shave before I was whisked through the streets of Lisbon by the same fast car to the airport. And so on to a civilian plane for London.

A few hours later I was ringing at the familiar door of Flat No. 10.

# Chapter 9

# Christmas Leave

I went on leave for a couple of weeks, which I spent with Father and Mother at Isleworth. Fitchell had arrived back in London safely, and two or three days after his return, both Major Y. and Paddy, making their way back by different routes, arrived. Fitchell and I had beaten them to it. My parents were glad that I was home again, if only for a short spell. I continued the pretence that I was still a War Office interpreter, dropping one or two hints that I might be going overseas, probably Cairo. I wanted to prepare them against the time when I would be out of England for a long spell. I had a feeling in my bones that the future would see me on some job abroad. The Middle East, Burma, or it might be somewhere across the other side of the world.

My father and mother often expressed hopes for my safety and welfare, and their obvious thankfulness that I was being kept out of danger, through their prayers to God, aroused in me only a feeling of revulsion. I found the devout atmosphere of the house at Isleworth stifling, Mother's religious views seemed to me childishly unreal. Her blind faith in God who would shelter her beloved son from the storm of war, and her profound certainty that He was on the side of Good, as represented by France and her Allies, and that He would bring about the destruction of the evil forces of Hitlerism, quite sickened me – though I kept my feelings to myself.

It was the same when my father talked about the wonderful world we were all going to live in after the war, when the Nazis had been wiped out and the Democracies would start afresh, with the good God to guide them. It seemed to me from personal experience, combined with what I was aware was taking place - the bombing of cities, the killing and maiming - that it was absolutely the stupidest way to start rebuilding the world. I thought of strong, keen-minded chaps like March-Phillips, who would not be there to enjoy the marvellous future awaiting us when the death and destruction ended. And there would be the old and unfit, the politicians with their incessant yattering over the radio; there would be the woolly-witted priests with their zealous appeals in the name of God, Jesus Christ the Saviour of Mankind, to one half of the human race to wipe out the other half of the human race, Amen.

These were not very original thoughts of mine; my ponderings were not reaching very deep down; my philosophy was probably twisted and full of over-simplifications. But my reaction to the Church and its message to a world torn with horror and death was one of utter disbelief and disgust. My way of escape from the dilemma which haunted and tortured me was the obvious way which was being taken by many of my comrades. It was not a very uplifting way. It did not solve the problem that vexed our innermost souls.

But where could we find the answer, except in the arms of a woman, or in drink?

Back to Blandford, where the feeling in the air was not calculated to salve raw nerves or soothe troubled minds. It seemed that the War Office top brass had reached the important conclusion that the job Appleyard and March-Phillips had been doing was producing results. The Nazis were taking our raids along the coast of Occupied Europe seriously.

Apart from their nuisance value – enemy posts along the coast were jittery and apprehensive of when the next blow from the dark sea would strike – we were bringing back a mass of useful intelligence. For example, the reports that Major Y., Fitchell, Paddy and I delivered after our trip across France brimmed with news about the morale of the Resistance, the Vichy people, those in Occupied France, and information relating to the Nazis' problems and plans.

And so now the brass-hats wearing out their bottoms on their chairs in the War Office were waking up to our usefulness. Their reaction was to demand more of the same sort of thing, and to this end they created a set-up headed by a colonel, whose first move was to gather a staff of Intelligence types around him and bring them down to Blandford, where they sorted out the problems for themselves. Personally, I decided that as Intelligence officers they were not marked by intelligence, and anyway, of course, they had absolutely no experience of the kind of warfare we had been operating.

Though a lot of us did collect a bit of a chip on the shoulder about it, I must say I could not have cared less. I was sent off with a few chaps and a sergeant, and Y. as my commanding officer, to another inevitable rambling old manor house near Redruth, in Cornwall. Here our job was to open one of the several new schools, which the War Office were starting for teaching this new style of operation.

My job was to train pupils in the use of small arms and put them through the assault-course, which Major Y. and I dreamed up ourselves, and it was as tough as we could make it.

It was a little while after I had arrived on this new job that I met Diana. She had been a 1939 debutante, her family were rolling in money, and in order to dodge being called up she had taken a farm near our training school. Her sister, who was several years older and a trouser-wearing, short-haired lesbian type, possessed of a vocabulary of four-lettered words, which had to be heard to be believed, ran the farm with Diana, and did all the work. Diana spent most of her time loafing about in bed, listening to gramophone records of jazz music. In her more energetic moments she drove an M.G. sports-car, as if she was competing in a race.

It was the sports car which gained me an introduction first to the sister and then to Diana. I thought I would call at the farmhouse to see if I could buy some fresh eggs on the quiet. I found the sister working on the M.G. in the farmyard, using the filthiest language as she tried to cope with whatever had gone wrong. I burst out laughing, and she looked up and shouted: "Well, why don't you give me a four-letter hand? Instead of four-letter word well standing there, four-letter word laughing at me?" The strange thing about her was that she never swore in front of Diana, and I never heard Diana use that kind of language.

In answer to the sister's choicely expressed request, I was helping with the car when Diana appeared. She was tall, blonde, with a wonderful skin. A typical English beauty, with a thin, high-bridged nose. She was twenty-four. That was the beginning. Pretty soon I was over there whenever I could get away, playing the gramophone to her, or roaring round the place in the M.G. Sometimes the girls' parents would come down for week-ends, and boy-friends, Guards officers, or R.A.F., or Royal Navy types, would come down on leave. And there would be girl-friends for her sister, very pretty some of them were, always fluffy and very feminine. I used to keep away from the farm when there were the chaps around, for I did not like pretending to them about my job. But sometimes Diana, who never asked me, or seemed to care what I was doing in that part of the world, would insist that I came over for a party.

It was late November, after one of these parties, when everyone was filled up to the ears with champagne, that I found myself in Diana's bedroom, and she had not got a stitch of clothes on. She told me to put out the light and draw back the curtains. A bomber's moon was shining, and the room was quite bright. It was about two o'clock in the morning. Diana looked marvellously white in the moonlight. I had known her nearly three weeks.

Looking back now, I feel that I can put my finger on this *affaire* with Diana as the turning point which was to direct me along the slippery road to the abyss into which I was destined to sink. This is not to say that I ever attach any hint of blame to her, or to anyone else. I was only a kid, it is true, but I knew right from wrong, and I deliberately chose to follow my dark star. Perhaps, if Diana had been an ordinary sort of girl, leading as rational a life as could be led in war-time, it would have made a difference to me; I do not know. But Diana was utterly spoilt and selfish, with more money than was good for her. Out for a good time, come hell or high-water. It astonished me what a good time could be had although a global war was raging. All you needed was the money to pay.

Certainly, to Diana and her crowd war restrictions were just a joke. I do not think I ever saw so much fresh butter and eggs, juicy steaks, and other luxury foods, not forgetting the drinks – whisky to champagne – that flowed freely, as I did at the farm-house, or when we went, as Diana and I sometimes did, to stay at her friends' homes.

At first it used to sicken me, I used to try to remind Diana what other people were suffering; starving, under-nourished millions of them all over the world. Her reply was always cynically logical: "If you don't have the stuff, darling, someone else will. So, it might as well be you." Once we spent a week-end with a well-known actress, famous for her patriotic songs and sentiments. She was always telling her audiences to grin and take it, until the day came when Britain would be dishing it out. If only those who listened to her could have seen how she herself lived. What she could not get in the black market, and it was little there she missed, she got from America. Food, drink, smokes, clothes, nylons, perfumes – bottles of it, together with jars of make-up and face-creams crowded her bedroom dressing-table – everything she wanted she had.

I began to subscribe to Diana's and her friends' philosophy. I began to believe that, even in the middle of this terrible holocaust, there was one code for the rich and powerful, and one for the poor under-dog, the bombed-out and homeless, the rank-and-file serviceman. The time of tension, the complete lack of security about what tomorrow might bring, all this encouraged those about me to feel and act as they did. If only I had been able to cling on to faith in God, as my parents would have had me do! Could I only have followed the example shown by men like Appleyard, for instance.

God-fearing, faithful to his belief in the triumph of goodness, scornful of the chap whose thoughts forever ran to women and booze; Appleyard and his kind sought their escape from the tension and horror of their job in prayer and meditation, poetry and music, the loveliness and peace of Nature. I could have gone along with them. I chose the other way.

And so, the next three months passed. I quite enjoyed training chaps to shoot down their fellow-men before their fellow-men shot them; or blowing human beings to bits; or to behave like apes, surmounting ingeniously devised obstacles, and wading through mud and slush, fire and water like exhausted maniacs. The rest of the time I spent with Diana and her friends.

It was just before Christmas, 1942, that I suddenly realized I was no longer praying before I went to sleep, or when I got up in the morning. I tried to recall when I had consciously stopped doing this, but I could not.

Diana and I went to London for my Christmas leave. I had written Father and Mother that my War Office job was going to keep me busy over Christmas. Diana and I stayed, as man and wife, at the Ritz Hotel. We occupied a luxurious suite, all gilt and plush. It was the night before Christmas Eve when we arrived, and as I unpacked my things I discovered I had not brought my rosary with me. In the hurry and excitement of packing I had forgotten it. Diana saw the expression on my face. "You look as if you've just found sixpence and lost a fiver, darling." I did not tell her what it was I had lost.

After dinner, the party Diana and I were with joined up with another in the bar, then we all went on to a night-club. It was hot and stuffy, in some basement off Regent Street, and we found ourselves a dark corner in the jam-packed place. The chaps and girls on either side of Diana and me were soon pawing over each other in the darkness, but Diana and I preferred to watch the cabaret. Diana hated public love-making. While a lot of nearly nude showgirls paraded about and a pansy sang at the piano, my thoughts kept going back to my parents, asleep at home in Isleworth.

"Bored, darling?" Diana asked me. "Shall we go back to the Ritz?" She took a look at the entwined figures sprawled on either side. "We shan't be missed." I had the strange notion that, if I could get away alone, I would go to Isleworth. I had the idea of just standing outside my home, while Father and Mother were sleeping inside. It was a guilty conscience I had about them, I suppose.

The winter's night was cold in our faces as we waited for the commissionaire to get us a taxi. All the way to the Ritz I tried to think of some excuse I could make, so that I could slip off to Isleworth. By the way she was clinging to me in the taxi I knew what Diana had in mind for the rest of the night, and she would take it badly if I tried to leave her even for an hour.

At the Ritz there was a message for me. A 'phone call from the manor house in Cornwall. A telegram had arrived there. It was in code from Appleyard. I was to report at Flat No. 10 at once. It was nearly two in the morning. The 'phone message had come through five hours earlier. I told Diana I had urgent orders to report to the War Office. "Too late to do anything about it now," she said. "Anyway, it's Christmas."

She made a bit of a scene when I said I had to obey orders – even if it was late. Even if it was Christmas. But there was nothing she could do about it, and there was nothing I could do about it, except get to Flat No. 10 fast. I said I would be back in an hour. I left her watching me sulkily through the swing doors of the Ritz. All thoughts of Father and Mother at Isleworth vanished from my mind; I waved to Diana and hurried off into the black-out. I did not know that I should never see her again.

Appleyard had not yet gone to bed when I arrived at the flat. To my surprise Y. was in the office. We grinned and wished each other a Merry Christmas. He had come up from Cornwall that afternoon, he said. There was that familiar air of purposefulness about Appleyard. He looked thinner than when I had seen him last. His eyes seemed less brightly blue. Like the shadow of prison bars across a prisoner in his cell, the shadow of March-Phillips' death still lay across Appleyard. He made no comment when I explained to him the reason for my delay in reporting. The office desk was strewn with maps and papers. Major Y. looked at Appleyard as he gave me a cigarette. I lit it and he lit his own, and he sat back in his chair. He glanced at me with slightly quizzical look, he knew I was impatient to know what it was all about, and he was enjoying keeping me in suspense. "They tell me that 62nd Commando isn't what it was," he said. "What d'you think? Or d'you enjoy it, being a school-teacher?" I shrugged. Then, without changing his casual tone, he said: "End of term for you, anyway. I've got a job for you in North Africa."

# Chapter 10

# Algiers

Appleyard told me that Y. and I would be leaving London that day. He was not accompanying us then, but would come out to North Africa later. I went back to the Ritz to pack and to explain to Diana what had happened, and that it was *au revoir.* I was not looking forward to the sort of scene which I anticipated my news would spark from her. I could have saved my anxiety on this score. Diana was not at the Ritz. I assumed that, fed-up with me for leaving her, she had returned to the night-club. There was no message. I was rather glad she was not there, it made it easier. I packed quickly, and after I had written Diana a letter, I returned to Flat No. 10. It was extraordinary how the prospects of action and excitement blotted her from my mind. Even as I left the hotel, the memory of her and all that she had meant in my life was fading.

I went to Isleworth to spin my father and mother a tale about being promoted to a cushy job in Algiers, that I was going out there by plane, and that I would be as safe as houses. Mother cried a bit, but I was full of excuses for not being able to stay long, and I was soon back at Flat No. 10.

That night Y. and two other chaps, both sergeants, and I caught the train for Liverpool. A couple of days later we left in a troop-ship, crowded with troops North Africa bound. It was after the Alamein campaign and a defeated Rommel had withdrawn his Afrika Korps into Tunisia. The Allied build-up, which was going to throw Rommel out of North Africa for good and all, was under way.

The voyage was uneventful. About two weeks' after leaving Liverpool we reached Algiers, warm and inviting in the Mediterranean sunshine after chill and wintry Liverpool. I was amused when our ship docked, at the speed with which Y., the two others and I were allowed ashore. We were first off, even ahead of the top brass aboard. That was one thing about being a special agent, no questions are ever asked you by your own authorities about passports or anything like that. No formalities at all. It is as if you are such a source of embarrassment to the official and red-tape types that they can hardly wait to get rid of you.

Special Service headquarters was a beautiful white villa, with palm trees and a shady garden, just outside Algiers, at a place called Cap Matifou. Here I was surprised and glad to meet Captain D. again. He was a major now, and was running things in France and Algiers. Easier to keep contact with agents from there than from London, he said. The four of us were not going to be allowed the tranquil delights of the villa for long. Next morning, we were off by lorry. We were joined by a bunch of chaps who were to work with us. They included several Frenchmen, a Hungarian named Sabo, who had been in the Foreign Legion, and an Arab, Sergeant Abdel Ahmid. Our job would be to work as infantry scouts behind the enemy lines; we brought the experience gained on our Commando raids, to impart to the others, who in turn gave us the benefit of their experience in their own type of unorthodox warfare. We stopped for the night at Constantine, a picturesque, ancient city, placed high up on a chalky rock. It was a railway junction for Algiers, Biskra and Tunis. The Americans had built an airfield there. Next morning, we pushed on in our lorry.

Now it was the front line next stop.

Our exact destination was a village named Beja on the single-track railway line between Algiers and Tunis. Our headquarters were the railway station, which was without doors or windows and with a dirt floor. Trenches surrounded it, and the area all round was well land-mined. Here our numbers were added to by a bunch of Communists, who had fought in the Spanish Civil War. They were a tough lot, and had already seen plenty of action.

Rommel was using agents behind our lines, naturally, but was employing the local Arabs for the purpose. A lot of Arabs were only too ready to act as spies against the Allies in the belief that, if we were kicked out of North Africa, the Nazis would give Tunisia back to them. These Arab agents were not in German uniform, and we had orders to shoot as a spy and without trial any Arab caught. We were to catch several of them during our night-patrols behind the enemy's lines. In the no-man's-land between Beja and Rommel was a small farm owned by an old Arab, and from whom we used to buy eggs and bread. He had three sons and a little grandson, and they often served us when we went to the farm. I used to talk a lot to each of the three sons, all of whom had been educated at the Paris Sorbonne and spoke perfect French.

One night I was leading a small patrol out of Rommel's lines, and as we headed for the railway station we suddenly heard a horse moving quietly through the darkness behind us. We waited and then jumped out on the rider as he went past. In the light from a torch I saw that it was one of the old Arab's sons. Even if we had not known what he had been up to the look in his eyes was enough. He was a spy. There was nothing for it but to settle his fate there and then, but I could not do it myself. I gave my orders in English, so that he would not understand me, and he was dragged off. The echo of the revolver shot seemed to reverberate in the desert darkness.

Three nights later, out on patrol again, we caught the first man's brother making his way on foot quietly from the enemy's direction. He was the father of the little boy. This time I could not duck my responsibility so easily; we were too near the enemy to attract their attention by a revolver shot, so I ordered our prisoner to be taken back to the railway station. It was all over very quickly, a couple of the chaps pushed him against the wall and I put one bullet into his head. All the time I could see his little son, dark-eyed and laughing, when I gave him chocolate and patted his head.

A short while later we were driven out of the railway station by Rommel's tanks and artillery, but only for a brief time. Our troops were sent up to counter-attack, and the railway station, or what was left of it, which was mostly smouldering ashes, was in our hands again. The very same day Major Y. told me that he, one of the sergeants (who had made up our original quartet), named Monty, and I were to slip some ten miles behind the enemy lines that night. Our objective: the German tanks, which had driven us out of the railway station, and which were now re-grouping. Once we had located them, Monty, who carried a radio-transmitter, would get in touch with our own artillery. The rest would be up to them.

It was just getting dark when the three of us set off, our pockets filled with chocolates and raisins, and carrying full water-bottles. Just after we had started it began to rain. It was the very fine rain which often fell at night that time of the year. The ground became slippery and treacherous in the darkness, and to add to our discomfort, shells from the artillery of both sides whined monotonously overhead.

Four in the morning showed on my wrist-watch when we finally located the tanks. We had crept down into a valley, and although we could not see very much, we could hear the sound of the tanks moving into position. We decided to wait until daybreak, so that we could obtain an exact picture of the target, to pass on to our gunners. We found a clump of tall grass and lay down there. In the darkness we could hear more tanks arriving. Obviously, they were building up for another attack.

At daybreak we had a clear view of the enemy armour, and Monty got busy radioing the exact number and position back to our artillery. The tanks were grouping down in the valley and we were about two hundred yards away above them. Just behind us we located a mine-field. Major Y. and I crept out of our hiding-place to scout round, and report back to Monty, as more and more tanks appeared up the valley to join the others. It was a little later when the balloon went up, as our artillery opened fire, while we continued to direct it from our hiding-place. We were able to report back the accuracy of the fire, as we saw tank after tank go up in flames and smoke. It was about midday when we decided we had completed our job, and that it was time to make tracks back to home and beauty sleep. The three of us were dog-tired, although we had taken it in turns to try and doze off during the night.

We stole out from our hiding-place, intending to make a detour, skirting the mine-field which barred the route back we had decided to take. As we came through some tall grass we stopped dead. Opposite us on the other side of the minefield stood an Afrika Korps type staring straight at us. We could see the grin on his face as he moved off round the minefield to report his discovery to a patrol. We dared not shoot him for fear of attracting attention. Our only chance was a short cut across the mine-field, there and then and fast. It was a hell of a risk, but better than waiting there until the enemy caught up with us.

Just as we left the grass to chance our luck, from out of nowhere appeared an Arab. He was running and fell almost on top of us. As he got to his feet he looked across in the direction the German had taken, and his mouth opened. Before he could shout out I stuck my commando knife into his back. The blow was not immediately fatal, and the Arab let out a terrible scream of agony.

"Run for it," I said to Y. and Monty, and, as they dashed across the mine-field, I let the Arab have it again, cutting short his scream to a brief gurgle. There was a lot of blood everywhere. By that time enemy rifle-fire, machine-guns and mortars had opened up on where Y. and Monty had been, and where I still was. I plunged off after Y. and Monty, bullets and mortar shells flying all around. Every few yards I had to throw myself flat on my face as the enemy fire got closer. Miraculously I escaped both the bullets and the mortar-shells, and avoided detonating any of the mines. It was possible to spot the metallic glint which betrayed the presence of a mine buried in the sand and to avoid it, but I was in such a hurry to escape the enemy fire I had no chance to pick my way. It was just luck on my side.

Major Y. and Monty had made it safely, and had gone into hiding when they had reached the other side of the mine-field. They were nowhere to be seen, and I carried on over the crest of the hill, keeping an eye open for the other two and for somewhere in which to lie low. It was Monty who saw me first; he and Y. had been on the look-out for me. They had stumbled upon a slit-trench, which though it was only shallow, was the best that could be found. I joined them in the trench. I was caked in a mixture of the Arab's blood and mine-field sand, and there the three of us remained crouched for the rest of the day.

The Afrika Korps chaps were searching for us all over the place. We could hear them shouting and yelling, but luck stayed along with us, and at last they called off the search. But our troubles were not yet over. Although the Germans had failed to find us they had not given up attempting to stop us getting back to our own lines. They knew what we had been up to in the valley, that we had been responsible for the destruction of their tanks. They did not like us getting away with that, and also to return with more information to be used against them. For the rest of that day mortar-fire was directed all over the vicinity of our trench. We dare not leave and make a dash for it; that would have been the signal for an inescapable concentration of rifle-fire and machine-gun bullets. So, they hunted for us, blindly, with mortar-shells, but failed to find us.

Shortly after 21.00 hours, as the moon was rising, we crept out of the trench. We could barely move with cramp and our limbs were stiff from our clothes, which had become rain-soaked the night before. But we edged our way forward, thankful for the silence around us, after the incessant clamour of explosions during the day, and fervently hoping the silence would not be broken by our discovery by the enemy. In our hurried departure from our clump of grass we had lost our maps, and the direction we were now taking brought us up against more mine-fields. The first one we took it in turns to lead the way across, each following behind carefully, walking in the leader's foot-prints. Since we could take our time, we could detect the warning glint in the moonlit sand, and so dodge past the mines.

We encountered and crossed three mine-fields without mishap, as we wandered as best we could towards the English lines. At last we reached our last obstacle, a muddy river. We were desperately tired, but summoned up enough strength to half-wade, half-swim across. We were stumbling upon several corpses, and decided we had reached the scene of a skirmish between one of our patrols and an enemy force.

Then we heard voices approaching, and promptly threw ourselves flat, burrowing into the sand in the hope that we ourselves might be mistaken for the dead. It would be just too bad if, after all that we had gone through, we should be picked up by Nazis' returning to their lines. As the voices grew louder we heard a few good old English swear words being used. It was in fact some of our own stretcher-bearers picking up wounded, so we called out and staggered over to them. They directed us the quickest way to an outpost, where we waited for a jeep from Beja to fetch us.

Back at our headquarters I went off to sleep as if I had been hit with a sledge-hammer. I did not wake up until midday. I went to see how Monty and Y. were feeling; Monty, who was very tall and fair, was very perky and pretty well recovered from the effects of our little trip. But I received a terrible shock when I saw Y. He had been dark-haired, but now his hair had gone quite grey. I had heard of people's hair going white overnight through shock or extreme suffering, but I had always thought it was an old wives' tale; now I knew that it could be true.

Grey hair or not, Y. and I were off with another patrol again that same night. This time our object was a small farm owned by an Arab in a village in no-man's-land, just in front of Rommel's lines. The farmhouse was convenient for German patrols, who came out to it for food. Our orders were to wait until the Germans were in the village, and then set fire to it and shoot everyone, German or Arab, as they tried to escape the fire.

None of us had much stomach for shooting down men, women and children, even if they were Arabs, and all of them capable of betraying us to the Nazis. It was not our idea of war. However, those were our orders. As well as wiping out the Germans as they came out of the fired village, we also aimed to take one or two of them alive for the usual interrogation purposes.

That afternoon Y. and I and the other seven of us detailed for the operation were studying maps. There were three pathways leading to the farmhouse from the German lines, any of which the patrol might use. We decided to split up into three lots of three, Monty and Sergeant Adbel Admid coming with me. Our information was that Rommel's chaps were expected at the farmhouse that night, between eleven and midnight.

It was just dusk as we set off; we had about five miles to go, so we got a lorry to take us part of the way. We were all pretty tired and our nerves on edge, we had been on the job during the past three months, ever since we had arrived at Beja; now the reaction was beginning to set in. We had heard that we should soon be off on leave to Algiers. But even that prospect failed to cheer us then. So, we were grateful for being able to travel some of the way by lorry, instead of foot-slogging it through the usual rain.

It was April 1943, and quite cold, which also helped to lower our spirits, together with the knowledge with what we had to do: killing Arab women and kids. Despite the drizzle we foresaw little difficulty in setting fire to the village huts with the specially prepared fire-bombs we had brought along with us. I felt sick to the stomach about the whole business. I had a nasty feeling that God was definitely not going to be on our side tonight.

It was about 21.00 hours when we crept up upon the village and separated to watch the three paths along one of which the enemy must come. A sergeant-major named Pastor, a peacetime motor-business man from Chad, and two others, took the farthest path; Y. and his chaps took the centre – and Monty, Abdel Ahmid and I the nearest path. The three of us spread out along the path, moving like shadows. We knew we hardly dare risk a whisper for fear our voices might carry to any suspicious Arab wandering in the vicinity. And so, we waited there in the darkness, the silence disturbed only by a dog barking in the distance, and the rattle of machine-gun fire: the Afrika Korps putting in some night-shooting practice.

Major Y. had decided that we should all give it till 06.00 hours, and if nothing had happened by then, we would return to our rendezvous with the lorry.

At about 02.00 hours, we heard whispers and saw figures approaching us out of the shadows and into the moonlight. This was it. We lay there tensed and waiting for the unsuspecting patrol to pass us on its way to the village; that would be the moment for us to signal the six others and to carry out our plan. Suddenly there was a Sten gun burst, followed by yells and shouting in English. It was not the enemy patrols, but Y. and his two chaps being fired at by Abdel Ahmid, who had mistaken them for Rommel's men.

What had happened was that Y., edgy and bored with waiting, had called it a day, and had come in search of me to advise me that we should all get back to the lorry. A bullet from Ahmid's burst had caught him in the fleshy part of the shoulder, and he would almost certainly have been killed had not Abdel Ahmid's gun jammed.

The firing and shouting set all hell loose, shouts and clatter from the Arab village, and the inevitable mortar-fire and machine-gun bullets from the enemy lines. There was nothing else we could do except get out fast, and we did. I patched up Y.'s shoulder as best I could. He was not badly wounded, but was losing blood and suffering from shock.

Sergeant-major Pastor and his chaps had also joined up with us as we headed for our rendezvous. There was no lorry, of course, since we had not planned for it to be there before 14.00 hours. So, we huddled together, cold and soaking wet and tried to cheer up Y.

The minutes dragged like hours, and all the time we were apprehensive that an Arab might sneak past and give us away to the Germans, who would quickly send out an overwhelming force to deal with us. However, we were not disturbed, our lorry arrived on time, and thankfully we went back to Beja.

Always before, when one of our operations failed to come off, it had always brought with it a feeling of anticlimax and depression. But this time as we trundled back through the grey light of the desert morning, a feeling of elation communicated itself from one to another. It was a feeling of relief; we had not had to carry out the bit about shooting down those Arab women and children like mad dogs.

When we reached headquarters, Y. was sent back to Algiers. A day or two afterwards I received news that he would not be returning to us anymore. From what I could gather, his experience of the past few weeks, culminating in the shock of the shooting, had left him washed-up, at any rate for some time. As his second-in-command I automatically took over, and during the next few days led a number of patrols, most of which were pretty successful. We had several narrow escapes, but we managed to get away with it, and also managed to kill a few of Rommel's chaps and bring one or two in for interrogation.

We had been provided with a mascot by now, someone had picked it up somewhere, a tortoise, which travelled everywhere with one of us, either in a pocket or tucked inside a shirt. His presence, we were all firmly convinced, was what accounted for our continued good luck.

One morning at our Beja headquarters I was told that a monk wanted to see me. I had heard of a religious order, who were known all over North Africa as the White Monks; they were evangelistic monks, and their missions did great work. They had a large monastery not a great distance away, in the middle of the desert. It was from there that this monk had come to offer, misguidedly it seemed to me, to take up arms in the cause of France. He was young and bearded, with dark eyes blazing with religious zeal. He was dressed in the white robes of a novice of his order, with a white rope round his waist, and he was wearing sandals.

"But you are a man of God," I argued with him, when he told me what he wanted to do. "What should you be doing fighting, killing people?"

"It is not a question of fighting as a man," he answered me fervently. "It is a question of taking part in a crusade for God against Evil."

Despite this sort of talk, which he put forward sincerely enough, I told him that it was his job to get back where he belonged, his monastery. There, let him pray that God would triumph and the Nazi evil would be defeated. "If prayer means anything at all," I said, "then your prayers will be answered, and you will be doing more good than you would be doing fighting alongside us."

What happened to him I do not know, but I certainly sent him packing. To me it was all wrong that a man of God should think of joining up to kill other men. I could not believe that he could possibly do the things we had been ordered to do. For instance, how would he have reacted to orders to shoot people trying to escape from a burning village, old men, women and children? I had not told him that this was the sort of thing he would have to do, that this was how the Allies would see to it that God would triumph over Evil. I was too ashamed to tell anyone these things. Easy enough for those sitting at their desks behind the lines to issue orders such as the one we had received. Not so easy for us, who had to steel ourselves against the horror of what we were ordered to do, and obey.

It was that morning, after the White Monk had left, that news came through that we were going on leave next day. But we had barely time to begin to enjoy the joyous prospect of all that gay Algiers had to offer us, when I received orders to take out a patrol that night to intercept an enemy lorry-convoy, which would be sneaking its way through a pass in the hills in no-man's-land to reach Rommel's lines. It was expected that there would be a score of lorries, and our job was to blow as many of them as we could off the face of the earth. The convoy would be well armed, and I knew our chances of getting away with it were slim. We might succeed in doing the convoy no good at all, but by the time the German armour had finished with us we should be lucky if any of us returned to tell the tale. When I told Monty, Abdel Ahmid, Pastor and Sabo, and the others, about the little trip we had to do, I could see it in their faces what they were wondering. How many of us would be on our way next day for that longed-for leave?

For myself I had a feeling that I should not be seeing Algiers after all. Of course, we all kept our spirits up by talking about the wonderful time we were going to have in Algiers. But I could detect the edge to my own voice as well as that of my comrades, the high note in our laughter. Our nerves were near snapping-point; we should have gone on leave long ago.

Since I had taken Y.'s place and was in command, I took my new responsibility very seriously. I decided I might help our plan to deal with the convoy effectively, and with as little loss to ourselves, by taking a look at the scene where we proposed to make our attack on the enemy. That evening, at 18.00 hours, I went by jeep alone into no-man's-land, out to a hill which I knew overlooked the route along which the convoy would pass that night. Leaving the jeep at the foot of the hill and taking my Sten gun with me, I climbed up to the hill-top. Suddenly I ducked down behind some rocks. Below me I could see half a dozen of Rommel's chaps out on patrol; they were going single file in the direction of their own lines.

They had not spotted me, and I had got them nicely in my Sten gun's range. All unsuspecting they moved quietly in the clear light of the evening. The sunset was beginning to redden the horizon that edged the desert and the pale, greenish sky, and each figure moved in its own strange aura. My hand shifted so that my finger squeezed round the trigger. The silence hung over the parched hill, the rocks and the desert. It was deathly still. Supernaturally still, as if everything was hushed before the silence was shattered by my Sten gun's burst of fire. But somehow, I found it impossible to fire, I could not break the awe-inspiring quiet, I could not kill that little handful of men below, so completely at my mercy. I waited until the patrol had disappeared from sight.

I carried out my observation of the place where the convoy of lorries would pass in the darkness, and decided how my patrol should best deploy itself. Then I found my jeep again and went back to headquarters. Arrived there, news was awaiting me that the operation had been called off. The lorry-convoy had been diverted, information had been received that the enemy force, for which the supplies were intended, had shifted the direction of its proposed attack. Together with these new orders, which lifted a dread load from all our hearts – now it was Algiers, here we come, for every one of us – I received news that I had been promoted to the rank of captain. When we returned to duty at Beja I should be commanding officer.

I was aged nearly nineteen.

# Chapter 11

# Surrender

We had arrived at Camp Robert, Constantine, in the early morning. We had travelled all through the night the three hundred miles from Algiers.

We had shot out of Algiers so fast that we had not had time to collect our mascot, the tortoise, from our villa garden, where we had parked it on our arrival several days before from Beja. Our mascot's absence was only a minor cause for our grumbling, as we had bidden a quick adieu to Algiers. As things turned out the tortoise was well out of it. Perhaps even to this day he is still nibbling happily away in that sunny garden of the beautiful white villa.

The job for which we had been sent so hurriedly, so hurriedly that the top brass had cut short our leave, required us to be parachuted about seventy-five miles behind Rommel's lines. We were going to use an American DC3. This necessitated special practice for the other chaps, since from this type of aircraft you had to jump through a side-door, instead of a trap-door in the floor of the fuselage. I was the only one who had experienced this way of jumping, and the idea was to spend a day or two at Camp Robert, practising from the DC3. It was on the last of these practice-jumps that I was to be involved in a bit of an accident, the first and only one I ever experienced parachute-jumping.

I had seen the others safely out of the plane and jumped last. We were flying at a very low altitude, and my 'chute opened a fraction of a second late, so that I was caught by the parachute of one of the other chaps opening slap in my face. Fortunately, my own parachute opened, or we might have both got entangled and dropped like stones, but the friction caused by the other 'chute burned my face and started my nose bleeding. However, I landed all right and was none the worse for what had happened.

As it turned out we might have saved our time practising with the DC3. When the Americans learned that our orders were to go over enemy territory alone and unescorted, they flatly refused to take us. They would fly us if their aircraft was given protection by other planes. A good old Halifax bomber was accordingly flown out to us from England; and the night after its arrival at Camp Robert was the night we planned to fly in it. The object of our operation was a railway junction on the Algiers to Tunis line, where a single-track line comes out from Sousse. We were to blow up the line at this point so that no petrol could get through to Rommel from the port of Tunis.

Our mission was to coincide with the Allies' all-out attack, which was to drive the Afrika Korps out of Tunisia into the sea. Tunis itself had been under Allied air-bombardment for the past two or three months, and Rommel was already desperately short of petrol, without which his armour could not move. Our big concerted attack, with the Americans in the south, the British in the centre and the French in the north, was timed for 16.00 hours the following morning. We were taking off in the Halifax some hours before at midnight.

We spent the hours preparatory to leaving studying maps, searching anxiously for any indication of cover wherein to hide after we had done the job; but all we could see, on either side of the seventy-five miles which we should have to foot-slog back to our lines, was arid desert, except for some fields of orange-trees a few miles distant from the junction. The charges we were to use to blow up the railway line would not explode until two hours after we had planted them. In those two hours we aimed to make ourselves scarce and head for the orange-fields, and there lie low for the rest of the day, leaving that night, to start on our return trip. If we were lucky we might hold up the first lorry that came our way and, pretending we were Italians, commandeer it. Sabo claimed to be able to speak sufficient Italian for our purpose, with only a slight Hungarian accent. The Americans' main contribution to our trip was their parachute uniforms, which were very practical, light and with plenty of pockets; and we also wore American battle helmets. These gave us some cause for amusement, since each had a cardboard lining which could be removed and worn to look like a helmet itself.

Midnight, and we got into the Halifax and settled ourselves on the floor, where we dozed or chatted away, Pastor and Sabo still expressing their fed-up feeling at not being back in Algiers. "Think of it," Sabo growled, "we should be having one helluva time at the Café de Paris, right at this very moment. Instead we are stuck up here in this damned Halifax." And while he and Pastor, with the others chiming in, began reminiscing about the wine and the girls they had left behind them, my own thoughts went back to that brief week or so of carefree days and nights, which had been whipped from us at such short notice. Days of sunning ourselves on the private beach of our villa, swimming in the warm, inevitable blue Mediterranean of that early spring of 1943; drowsy afternoons, lolling against the oars of a gently moving boat. And those hectic all-night parties at the Café de Paris.

Run by and staffed almost entirely by French people, the Café de Paris was Algiers' most glamorous caravanserai. It was more of an hotel, with softly-lit rooms upstairs to which customers could discreetly retire with their companions of the evening, and was just like a choice piece of Paris set down in the teeming, cosmopolitan city. The most alluring and expensive girls were to be found there, and from the moment we hit the town these blondes, brunettes and red-heads of half a dozen nationalities had no cause to complain of the lack of clients.

A dozen or more of us were there every night; besides my chaps and I from Beja, there were other special service types on leave, all of us with money to burn, and we used to fairly take the place apart. We would kick off the evening's entertainment with a terrific dinner-party, and the wine flowed, the music continued, with suitable love-making interludes, until the pale dawn crept in from the sea to wash the shadows of night away from the city and make it white and shining again for the new day.

One girl had made a dead set at me from the first night I had shown up there. She was very, very blonde, with light blue eyes, which went rather strangely with her sun-bronzed skin; she possessed the longest, slimmest legs I ever saw on a girl of only medium height; her accent was a mystery, though she told me she had been born in Cairo, of mixed French and Greek parents. She was amusing in a sharp, feline sort of way.

Perhaps one reason why I attracted her was that, apart from my money, she was intrigued by my own strength and virility. It was as if we were two wrestlers, seeking to overpower the other.

Then two nights before we were suddenly ordered to shake the dust of Algiers off our heels, the girl failed to turn up at the Café de Paris. I was expecting her, and made enquiries of one or two of the waiters, but no one had any explanation for her absence. It was not until later, when we were at Constantine, working with the DC3, that an American arriving from Algiers casually mentioned something about the nude body of a moonlight blonde, as he called her, having been fished out of the harbour in Algiers old town, near the Kasbah. It sounded so much like the girl I had known at the Café de Paris, that I questioned the American more closely. It was her all right. "A real-life Mata Hari, that was her racket," the American enlightened me. "Least that's what they say. But whose side she was on, don't ask me. Maybe both sides, maybe that's why someone dropped her in the drink."

I tried to recall anything about her the least bit suspicious. She had made no attempt to wheedle any secrets out of me. But it may have been that my hard-headedness, no matter how much wine I put away, made me a dubious prospect from an information point of view. Or perhaps she, too, was on leave – after all, even a spy must have a little fun – and she was enjoying a good time before she, too, went back on duty?

It was around 14.00 hours of our last night in Algiers, though we were blissfully unaware of the fact at the time, that a dispatch-rider roared up to the Café de Paris. He had orders for me to report back with my chaps to headquarters immediately. We were, until that moment, in the middle of what promised to be our wildest party to date. I had received official confirmation of my promotion to captain, and we made it the excuse – as if we had needed one – to outdo ourselves. I had been provided with a specially chosen girl for the night – an utterly uninhibited half-Spanish, half-Arab girl, very petite, with wonderful white teeth.

It took me a few seconds to get over the shock of the dispatch-rider's arrival and the orders he had brought. Then, when I was convinced it was not some practical joke that was being played on us, I went round sorting out the others who would be leaving with me. Not all of them were downstairs, and there were several embarrassing moments, although not without their funny side, as, accompanied by a couple of us who were not at the moment so preoccupied, I made the rounds of the upstairs rooms. Then we were off to the villa.

And now, here we were, setting out on another job, and the days in the sun and the hectic nights at the Café de Paris were a long way behind us. They might never have been.

After an hour's flying, the dispatcher came and informed us we were over enemy territory. We hardly needed to be told that, we could already feel the bump, bump of anti-aircraft guns firing at us. We were flying much too high to be in any danger.

Presently, back came the dispatcher to tell us to put our parachutes on, and we got ready. All our Sten guns and explosives were in containers, which would be dropped just before us. Now the trap-door was open and the Halifax began a wide circle. In the bright moonlight we could see the railway line glinting below, as it snaked through the desert. We were to be dropped about three miles from the line, and we would have to walk back to it when we got down. I took my bearing by my compass. We were all set.

The green light flashed above my head as the aircraft lost altitude and glided down. Now the red signal light showed, out went the containers, I felt the dispatcher's tap on my shoulder, and with a little grin at him out I went. All I had to do was to follow the containers down. I landed just beside them.

The pilot had in fact got the Halifax down a bit too much as we made our jumps. As I left the aircraft the revolver holster round my waist came undone and my revolver fell out, but I quickly found it again when I landed, which shows how low we were flying.

I landed without trouble, and was already starting to scoop out a hole in the sand to bury the parachute and harness, when the silence was shattered by a sudden commotion near at hand; dogs were barking and I could hear men shouting. By now the rest of us had jumped, and the Halifax was turning back for home. I went off with some of the others to see what had happened.

We found we were near – much too near – an Arab village, and Pastor, who had jumped last, had landed on one of the village huts and broken his leg. Several Arabs were clustered round him as he lay on the ground beside the hut, and they were kicking up a fine old noise. It was now past 14.00 hours, there was not much time to lose. The job came first, before anything else, even thought for your pal; the lives of troops, who would be thrown into the attack, depended on our success. Poor old Pastor was the first to agree that we leave him there in the Arabs' care. We gave them money and hoped they would hand him over all right to Rommel's men, who would treat him as a prisoner-of-war.

To be caught as we had been in the act of landing by the Arabs was all that we needed to put an end to our entire plan. We knew that within a very short time the enemy would be well aware of our arrival on the scene. However, I told Abdel Ahmid to tell the Arabs we were Germans, who had been forced to leave our plane in a hurry before it crash-landed.

I was not impressed by the Arabs' expressions, as they listened to Abdel Ahmid. They looked a damned disbelieving lot. So, we set off in the direction of the railway line. Apart from Pastor we had all landed safely. Monty had landed in some cactus, of which there were plenty in the vicinity, and his face was bleeding, but that was a mere trifle. We went along as quickly as we could, cursing the blessed pilot of the Halifax for dropping us so near the village.

By the time we arrived at the railway level-crossing, where we intended to plant our explosives, we found some Germans already there; they must have got wind of us and guessed what we were after. They were stopping all traffic on the road, which ran alongside the railway. We aimed to blow up the line five hundred yards on each side of the crossing. Now we would have to work right under the very noses of the enemy. But it was the sort of tricky operation we were used to. So, we divided up, and, singly or in pairs, each man laid ten charges, making seventy in all. The explosives had time-pencils attached and were set to go off two hours later.

Afrika Korps men kept milling around all the time, but they never spotted us as we moved like wraiths along the railway track, taking advantage of every inch of cover, every shadow cast by the moon. When we had finished we met up together at a pre-arranged point down the line to get our bearings before we started on the return journey. The entire job had taken us ten minutes to complete, and we were congratulating ourselves under our breath, when suddenly there was an almighty explosion. The ground shook beneath our feet. We looked at each other. Then came another and yet another; we knew what had happened. Some bloody idiot had made a mistake at headquarters and attached ten-minute time-pencils to the explosive, instead of two-hour ones.

The explosions were the signal for all hell to be let loose, someone began firing in our direction, and all we could do was answer their fire as we slowly withdrew along the railway line towards the road. Across the road lay the orange-grove, and that was where we had to get – if we could.

I cursed the beautiful night, under the bright moon, where every movement could be seen as if in broad daylight. As soon as we reached the road, we ran for it, heading in the direction of the orange-grove, the Germans hard on our heels. We would find a rough field into which we dashed, but always we came up against cactus, which turned us aside. Nowhere could we see any cover at all, and the orange-grove seemed as far off as ever.

I knew that unless we found cover of some sort before dawn broke the game would be up. After all the damage we must have done the Germans would be determined to get us. Then we came across a wide clump of nettles; the enemy had lost touch with us for the moment, and I decided that, however uncomfortable as our hiding-place, the only thing to do would be to get deep into the nettles, stick there for the day, and try to get away during the night. My watch said 19.00 hours, we were all in, and so we went into the nettle-clump and settled down with one on guard, while the rest of us slept.

I had fallen into an exhausted sleep, and then I was suddenly awoken by the chap on guard. "Look who's here," he said. In the distance I saw four armoured cars coming at full speed towards us. My watch said 20.00 hours.

I woke the others, and we watched the enemy come across the desert. Afrika Korps troops jumped down to the ground and circled our clump of nettles and began firing. This was the end. There was nothing for it but to surrender. Our job had been completed, no point in sitting here to be killed. Sick in heart, I gave the order to surrender; and getting up, leaving my gun on the ground, I went slowly towards the enemy. Tears of rage and humiliation were pouring down my face.

We were all disarmed and searched, and then, with our hands above our heads, we began the long journey into captivity.

As well as our guards, which included one of the armoured cars, trundling behind us there were about two hundred Arabs accompanying us. Where they had come from I do not know, but they followed us for the twenty-five miles we had to walk, calling us every name under the sun in French and Arabic. All along the road Arabs came out of their huts to give our captors water and food, always refusing us any.

Early that afternoon, on our last legs, we approached a place called Eil Gem. Just before we reached Eil Gem we saw a British aircraft fly over in the direction of the railway junction. It was taking photographs of the damage we had done several hours before. As I watched it fly away into the distance I wondered if I should ever see the world to which it was returning again; yet at the same time I felt immensely proud to think it would carry the evidence back that we had completed our mission.

On our arrival in Eil Gem, we were hustled into a small café, which was owned by a huge Frenchman, who shrugged at us as if to say there was nothing he could do to help us, and went about his business of serving his customers; the café was full of them. But now they were soon pushed out, the French proprietor, still shrugging his helplessness, retired to his kitchen. We were ordered to sit down at a table. We were each given a glass of beer and a hard-boiled egg to eat, while the Germans began on our concentrated chocolate, which they had taken from us, and our cigarettes. I hoped fervently that they made pigs of themselves over the chocolate, which was so concentrated, if you ate more than one or two pieces at a time, it made you very sick.

Then our so-called trial began.

It was presided over by an Afrika Korps colonel and his lieu-tenant. Everything we had in our pockets was laid on the table, including a knuckle-duster, which came out of someone's pocket, and sparked off a terrific burst of vilifications against us from the colonel. It was against the Geneva Convention to use such an offensive weapon, it was considered too offensive.

The farce ended early that evening, when, without being given a chance whatsoever to speak for ourselves, we were told that we had been convicted as saboteurs and would be shot the next morning. Not only were we saboteurs, but liars also, we were further informed – we had said we were British, but only two of us spoke English, and we all wore American uniforms. When sentence had been passed upon us, the colonel departed, the café was re-opened, and the customers came streaming back. Among them appeared a couple of Arabs, who came in to collect their money. Apparently, they had spotted us in the nettles and, for the price of a few measly cigarettes, had sold us to the Germans. We felt somewhat insulted to think that we were worth so little, especially as we had gathered that our little job at the railway junction had been a great success from our point of view, causing terrific damage to the railway line.

With the lieutenant in command, we were marched off to the local lock-up, and assigned a cell between the six of us. The last occupant had been an Arab, and he had obviously been given a rough going-over by his captors. The cell was filthy, and the walls and floors spattered with blood. The lieutenant refused to allow the gendarme in charge of the jail-house to clean the cell, and we were all shoved inside. We were allowed to have our water-bottles refilled, and when they were returned to us we discovered they had been filled with wine, probably by the gendarmes.

The cell itself had a cement floor, no windows, and was about six feet wide with a huge oak door, the only means of light and ventilation being a small hole in the roof. None of us spoke much; there were two guards outside the door, all ears, and, anyway, we were all far too busy thinking about the coming of the dawn and our execution.

Every hour a duty-officer came in to count us and see if we were all there – how he imagined we could get out I do not know, it was quite impossible to escape. I looked round in the gloom at my comrades, Monty, Sabo and Abdel Ahmid and the others, and wondered what they were all thinking about. I wondered how Pastor had got on, with his broken leg. By now, no doubt, he too would have been betrayed for the price of a few cigarettes. At about 05.00 hours, when it was still dark, they came to fetch us. We filed out of the cell, with our hands above our heads, between two rows of Afrika Korps chaps, carrying rifles and bayonets. We were pushed into a closed van, and had to sit, in silence and in the darkness, our hands still above our heads. The guards climbed in, and we were driven off. We knew where we were being taken to. We were on our way to our place of execution. We rode along in the van for about an hour, then we felt the road become very bumpy, as if we were backing into a field. Then the van slowed down. The van stopped.

The door opened and the dawn light blinded us.

This was it.

# Chapter 12

# Stalag Luft III

But it was not a grave freshly dug for us, nor a firing squad that met our gaze when our eyes became accustomed to the early morning light after the dimness of the van. Instead we found ourselves drawn up alongside a Junkers Ju 52. We were ordered to get into it, and we did. I was feeling a little less sick in the stomach; it seemed that we were not going to be shot, yet.

As I learned later, the local Nazi commander-in-chief had shrugged off carrying out the death-sentence, because of the Allied attack that was taking place at that time; so, as we were regarded as saboteurs and not soldiers at all, he had passed us and the responsibility for our execution over to the Gestapo. This meant that we were en route for Rome.

Our first stop was to be Naples, and we were going along with a flight of about twenty troop-carrying planes. The troops were led to believe that they were going home on leave, but in reality, it was the start of the evacuation of the Afrika Korps. Two weeks later the Allies had, in fact, conquered Tunisia. I hoped fervently that our own fighter planes would come along and shoot us down – the Germans had no fighter escort, and at least we might have had a chance of escape. To me, anything was better than captivity, any chance to escape was welcome. It did not occur to me that I might be killed if the Junkers I was in was attacked, all I thought of was the possibility of being able to do something to outwit the Nazis. We were not allowed to speak to each other, but I fancied I could tell from the looks on the others' faces that they were thinking the same as I.

We arrived in Naples as evening was falling, and we were led from the plane to the airport control-tower and shoved into a small room under guard by Luftwaffe personnel. We were left here for a couple of hours without food or drink. We had been given nothing to eat or drink since we left North Africa. Eventually we were taken to a hotel in Naples by lorry, there to spend the rest of the night.

We were filthy dirty and desperately tired, now the reaction of the past hours of tension and nerve-strain was beginning to set in, and we all felt terrible. We were put into two rooms, still heavily guarded, and given soap, towels and razors.

We washed and shaved, and, feeling a bit better, we were then taken into a dining-room; on the wall was one of the largest pictures of Hitler that I have ever seen. The room was full of officers, and each time they entered the room they paused by the picture to give the Nazi salute. The food was not very good, but we did not mind what it was like so long as it was food. After the meal we were taken upstairs to sleep.

At 06.00 hours we were woken up and, after breakfast, the next stage of our journey started. We were off to Rome. We went by train, and were very heavily guarded the whole way there. It was a military train, a corridor one. On the train we relaxed a bit, the guards were Korps chaps, and they brought us oranges, chocolates and soup. One youngster of only seventeen or eighteen told me he had been to England as a boy scout.

Arriving at Rome, we were met by a bunch of civilians, very young and smartly dressed, and not at all like the slit-eyed toughs we had expected. They did not look it, but they were from the Gestapo. There were about four or five, but behind them I saw a military guard, so there seemed to be little possibility of escaping our new hosts. The station was crowded with German and Italian troops, and I could not help smiling at the way the Germans and Italians yelled insults at one another.

Outside the station I caught a glimpse of the top of the Vatican roof and the silvery dome of St. Peter's; really lovely they looked with the sun shining on them and the bright blue sky behind. I wished fervently I could get away long enough to find sanctuary in neutral Vatican City.

Our lorry stopped in the yard of what appeared to have been barracks of some sort, and we were led into a room and told to undress completely, and give up everything we had. I was handed a pair of wooden shoes, worn French soldier's jacket, a pair of trousers and an old coat. Then I was taken away to a cell, and I found that I was to be in it alone.

My cell was about nine feet by ten; there was a stool and a pail in the corner, and that was all. A heavily barred window, glazed with glass so thick it was impossible to see through, and the whole time I could see the shadow of a guard moving up and down outside. There were no sheets on the bed, and on a little table was a spoon and a fork made of wood.

I soon discovered that the cell was centrally heated. The heat could not be turned off by me, and I began to feel uncomfortably hot. In the evening some food was pushed into me through a hatch in the door, a glass of water and something that was very strongly salted, and which made me feel thirstier and hotter than ever. My watch had been taken from me, but I suppose the time was about 18.00 hours. It was obvious that the central heating was kept on deliberately to make me sweat and thirst.

Suddenly one light in the ceiling of my cell went out, and there I was left in complete darkness, the heat growing more intolerable. Day and night for the next fortnight I lived in those conditions. I was not given either water for shaving or washing. The food never varied from day to day, coffee and some bread, and nobody ever spoke to me, and I sometimes felt myself in danger of going silly in the head. In order to occupy my mind, I used to pull straw out of my mattress with which to make crude sorts of toy airplanes and send them flying round my cell. I always slept on the floor as it was cooler.

After two weeks of this – it could have been night or day, I was past knowing or caring – a man came in. He was about sixty, bald and dressed in civilian clothes. He pulled a face at the stench; I had only the bucket in the corner to use for purposes of elimination, and it was not emptied until it was full to overflowing. "Ah, the bloody Germans they have caught you," he said. He told me he was a Swiss from Geneva and wanted me to tell him all about myself. I spoke to him in French, but he himself could speak no French, and I suspected that he was a Gestapo type. He handed me a form asking for all sorts of details about me. On the top of the form was the legend "Red Cross", as if to show it was genuine Red Cross document; but this portion was perforated so that it could have been torn off when I had completed it. I wrote down name, rank and number, which information I was allowed to give, anyway. After that I did not fill in anything else.

My visitor said that if I did not fill in any more my parents would never know what had happened to me, to which I replied that I was sorry. He then asked me what type of explosives we had used on the railway line job, so I realized that the Germans were in ignorance of how we had worked. He assured me he only wanted to know for his own edification, but I told him I could not satisfy his curiosity: it was against the rules of war for him to ask me. In the end he lost his temper and left the place in a hurry. He had shaken hands with me when he came in, but he did not shake hands when he left, taking his bogus form with him.

I lasted for another week in the same conditions. The heat, the stench, the thirst, the horrible loneliness. Then one day I was taken off by guards to an office where I was faced by a

parachute-regiment colonel. He was very good-looking in a typically Teutonic way, with slightly greying hair. He gave me my
very first cigarette since I had been captured. He spoke extremely
good English, and began to talk to me all about how he had lived
in Maida Vale before the war; his mother was English. He was
chatting casually about the Jews, how after the war they would
all be sent to Madagascar, and never be permitted to leave the
island – he said quite openly that he was a Nazi – and then his
manner changed and he suddenly asked me if I was a special
agent.

"I am a soldier," I replied. "I belong to the parachute-corps."

"First or second regiment?"

I had no idea, I did not even know if there were any parachute-corps in Africa. I replied that I was attached to the first regiment, and hoped for the best.

"Odd," he said, "we have prisoners from the second regiment,
but not from the first. Anyway, I am glad for your sake you are
not one of the special service men, you would have a much harder
treatment." I did not make any reply, but waited to see what he
would say next.

"If you are a parachute-officer," he went on, "you can have
trained in two places, either Ringway or Salisbury Plain."

I knew I should have to say one or the other, and so, knowing
Ringway and nothing about Salisbury Plain, I replied that I had
been trained there. He could not make me talk about a place I
knew nothing of.

"Which town did you go to in the evenings?"

I had no idea at all. "Salisbury?" he prompted me.

"Yes," I replied.

"Is the death ride still in Salisbury?" he said.

He was referring to a motor-cycling act at some place of entertainment, but I had never heard of the death rider. I thought he
meant a regiment, so I replied: "Yes."

That was all he got out of me. I learned from him that Tunis
had fallen to the Allies, and so possibly the papers about us which
the Germans there would have forwarded on might never come
through. As the Gestapo would have no definite information that
we had in fact been sentenced to death as saboteurs, we would
still be treated as soldiers. All that was known was that we had
been caught blowing up a railway line, which might have been a
military operation.

I had no idea what was happening to Monty, Sabo and the others all this time, but guessed that they, too, were giving nothing
away. I was stuck with the colonel for about four hours, talking

of nothing at all, and then suddenly firing a question at me. He continued to get nowhere at all fast, and so I was shown back to my cell.

Three days later I went through the same routine with him again. While he still failed to dig any more information out of me, I learned that the Gestapo were in fact unable to understand why the seven of us had been handed over to them. To their minds we were soldiers, and we should be dealt with by the military authorities.

From time to time I could hear some tapping on the wall of my cell, but I could not make out what the tapper was trying to convey to me – I had forgotten all the Morse I ever learnt. I never knew who it was in the adjoining cell. Though I used to knock back, I could not send a proper message. For all I knew it might have been a Gestapo plant trying to trap me into revealing something to him.

Then one day I received news that the seven of us were to be sent over to Germany. I was taken out of my cell and along to a room, where my six comrades and I had our clothes returned to us and all our belongings, which we had left with our captors. We were given a shower and got a shave. We were all pretty perky, and though we were not allowed to talk managed to exchange a few words between ourselves. It seemed that the Gestapo had decided that since we were parachutists, we were not army types, but airmen, and therefore came under the jurisdiction of the Luftwaffe.

We were taken to the railway station, and there handed over to a party of Luftwaffe officers and men, who had been with the Afrika Korps, and were going on leave for the first time in three years. We were en route for Frankfurt-on-Main, where there was a prisoner-of-war camp called Dulag Luft. The officer in charge, who spoke English quite well, told me his girl-friend was a nurse in Russia, and they always wrote to each other in English. Near Frankfurt-on-Main, he went on to say, he owned a castle. If I gave my parole not to escape, he offered to arrange for me to spend a week-end with him at the castle. He was very young and good-looking, and sounded as if he belonged to an aristocratic family. But I told him I was unable to accept this offer.

We occupied two compartments, with a Luftwaffe man on each side of us. Monty, Sabo and I were in one compartment, and the four others were next door. We had left Rome at about ten o'clock that evening, reaching Munich very early the next morning. Munich had been bombed heavily that night by the R.A.F. When Monty and I went along the corridor to the lavatory,

accompanied, as usual, by our guards, some civilians on the plat-
form saw the parachute-wings, which we were allowed to wear
as a cover for our real job, on our uniforms, they began beating
their fists on the windows and shouting: "Murderers." The officer in charge went out, and I heard him say to the people: "*Nicht
flieger, soldaten.*"

The train started again, and standing in the corridor were two
young girls. The officer asked them to come into our carriage,
while a couple of Luftwaffe men made room for them. One girl
sat next to me. She was very young, slim and about nineteen or
twenty. The other sat down beside Monty. The girl only spoke a
little English, and we did not talk to them very much at first.

We had been given some German rations before we left Rome,
sour bread and Italian bully-beef, a tin of which we presently
opened. It was horrible. None of us liked the look of the stuff,
and then the girl next to me took some white bread and ham from
her attaché-case, and she gave me half of her share. We began
talking, and, in her halting English, she told me she was working
in an ammunition factory in Munich, and she was going on leave.
When she expressed the opinion that the war was no good for
anybody, that it would be better if Hitler and Churchill fought it
out together, the Luftwaffe chaps laughed and agreed with her.

The train went through about five very long tunnels, and
each time the Luftwaffe officer directed the light from his torch
along the floor. He could see if our legs moved, if we showed any
intention to try to get away. By now the girl, whose name was
Hildegarde, had one arm round my waist and her head on my
shoulder. In the darkness of the tunnels no one could see us kiss
each other, and when we could not enjoy the protection of the
darkness of the tunnels, Hildegarde talked as best she could in
her inadequate English.

When she asked me if I had a sweetheart in England, and I said
I had not, she smiled as if she was pleased. She told me to go and
see her after the war. The girls left the train before us at Frankfurt-
on-Main. Hildegarde had wanted to give me her address, but I
told her that it might not be so good if her address was found on
me. She was very upset about that, but agreed that what I said
was best. She was crying when we said good-bye. I promised I
would remember her address and try to come to see her when the
war was all over.

Dulag Luft III was a tram ride distance from the railway station, and we were put on the tram, still with the guards who had
accompanied us on the train. Dulag Luft III was a transit-camp for
R.A.F. personnel. Here we were searched once more, our money,

pens and cigarette-lighters were taken away from us. Dulag Luft was entirely for R.A.F. prisoners: non-commissioned officers and other ranks. I had a shave and shower and then went along to a mess-room in search of some food. I ordered my six chaps to keep on the alert; we knew no one at the camp, and still did not know if we really were going to be put with genuine prisoners, or if the whole thing was a put-up job by the Gestapo.

A small chap with a red face and bald head came up to me and asked me where I had been captured, and what I was doing. I refused to answer, even when he explained that he was a clergyman who had been captured because he was carrying arms. Now I was told that because I was an officer I was to be separated from my comrades and sent to Stalag Luft III, later to become famous in Eric Williams' book, *The Wooden Horse*. Stalag Luft III was a camp for R.A.F. officers only, and I was still regarded as an airman, though I tried to explain that I was an Army officer. Nazi paratroopers were under Luftwaffe command, it was in turn explained to me, and there was nothing I could do about it.

So, at 18.00 hours the next morning I was on the train with a whole crowd of R.A.F. officers, including the padre, headed for Stalag Luft III. It was at a place called Sagan in Silesia, which is near the Polish border. Once again it was a corridor train, each compartment packed. Guards were at each compartment door and a machine-gun was at the end of the carriage.

We were in that train for three days and nights; each time a troop-train came past we were shunted into a siding. The thing which shook me was that while the Afrika Korps had been smart and very well-dressed, these troops from the Russian front looked like wild animals, their faces were thin and hollow. Many of them had no shoes, their feet were bound up in sacking. They looked like haunted men. At this time the Russians had launched their huge counter-attack, and the Nazis were in retreat. I was reminded of the fall of France; all the soldiers appeared silent and depressed-looking, as if they did not care what happened.

We finally arrived at Sagan, and as we marched through the town we passed a monument, which marks Napoleon's retreat before the Russians. The terrain all around Sagan was very flat, the ground was sandy and everywhere were pine trees.

It was in the middle of a pine forest that, through the trees, we saw Stalag Luft III. We went through great barbed-wire gates, and halted at the offices just inside, where I was photographed, given a number (mine was 923), which was used in all correspondence; my Army number did not count any more.

The whole proceedings made me feel as I imagined a convict might feel. When later I saw my photograph, and with my number on it, I looked exactly like a criminal. Finger-prints were taken in case I escaped, or if I was repatriated: according to the Geneva Convention I could not fight on the same front. Then the inevitable searching, and I was taken through another large gate, beyond which were the long, low, wooden huts.

I was a prisoner-of-war in Stalag Luft III.

# Chapter 13

# Thoughts of Escape

From the moment I arrived at Stalag Luft III the thought uppermost in my mind was how to get out. I felt nothing but contempt for the Kriegsgeffeners, or Kriegies, as we called those prisoners who had been there since 1941 and 1942, and had settled down to the monotony of prison life, some studying to be teachers, lawyers, or even doctors, or the more artistically inclined who fancied themselves as painters.

There were plenty of other prisoners who had the same idea as I, and there was an escape committee, whose chairman was known only to the half a dozen committee-members; to the rest of us, who never knew his identity, he was known as X. This security was one of the many measures taken to avoid the risk of anything being given away accidentally to our captors.

The prospects of escaping seemed utterly hopeless. All around the camp guard-towers had been erected on which were mounted search-lights and machine-guns. Guards were on the watch day and night. At night the search-lights inexorably explored every inch of the camp. There was an outer nine-foot barbed-wire fence right round the camp, and inside this a six-foot space filled with barbed wire in rolls, then another nine-foot inner barbed-wire fence. There was a twenty-five-yard no-man's-land all the way round, which was marked by a trip-wire. If you put one foot over this you would be shot without warning.

All the time, armed guards patrolled outside, and at night guards with Alsatian dogs roamed round inside the camp. Some of the escape ideas I dreamed up included the suggestion of of vaulting over both fences with a pole, but in practice they would have proved too high and too far apart. Next, I had the idea of a rope-ladder, which could be thrown over the fences, but that would have proved too noisy, and anyway there was still that no-man's-land to cross.

I shared a room in one of the low-built huts with the padre and two Australians. One was named Fraser, very boyish, fair and tall with a great sense of humour: and the other, who had been a journalist in peace-time, short and curly-haired with a little moustache, who was named Paul Brickhill. As soon as I had arrived at the camp I was given clothes by various Kriegies from their own belongings: pyjamas, shirts and shoes; so that although my wardrobe was a miscellaneous collection I was fairly warm and had a decent pair of shoes to wear.

Red Cross parcels used to get through quite regularly, but what used to disgust us was that the cigarettes in them hardly ever arrived. They were stolen in England before they even left for Geneva. We deduced this from the fact that we received all Canadian and, later, American cigarettes invariably intact. When my father eventually received news that I was a prisoner-of-war, he placed an order for me to be sent two hundred cigarettes a week, but in the two years that I was at Stalag Luft III, only one parcel got through to me complete with the cigarettes.

An item in the parcels which did interest me was playing-cards. I collected as many of these as I could; I had conceived the brilliant notion of scraping the celluloid substance off the cards. Celluloid was an explosive, and I used to put my scrapings into a sealed tube and try to set fire to it to prove this theory. The padre, Fraser, and Brickhill used to dash out of the room every time I produced my home-made bomb to test it, in case it did, in fact, explode. But somehow it never did.

I quickly fell into the prison camp routine. It was very necessary in a prisoner-of-war camp to maintain discipline and order, as more and more batches arrived, including American flyers; the camp held fourteen hundred men. There were twenty-four rooms to each wooden hut; each with its occupants' names and numbers on the door. Each room was furnished with four bunks, two on each side of the room, one above the other, and made of wooden planking. Also, a stove which was of little use, because we could not get enough coal to keep it going. We used to make our own stoves, much smaller, out of tins and fit them inside the big stoves.

There was a cooking-stove at the end of the corridor, which divided the rooms, where we cooked the main meal of the day. The rest of our meals consisted mainly of bread and spam. Next to the kitchen was a lavatory and washrooms; make-shift showers had been put up out of tins and lengths of piping which had been collected, but we had no hot water. We made our own alcoholic drink out of dried raisins and sugar – a combination so poisonous that excessive amounts could send you temporarily blind. The occupants of the different rooms saved up their sugar and raisins and threw parties.

When I first arrived at the camp I was regarded with some suspicion by my fellow-prisoners. To them I was an Army type, while they were all R.A.F., who knew each other, or had mutual friends, which provided them with an authentic background. And, of course, my French accent, plus the fact I was much too young to have been made a captain, added to the suspicion that I was in reality a spy planted there by the Nazis. The security set-up was run by a wing-commander named Stanford-Tuck – he interrogated me on my arrival, and I knew that I did not satisfy him with my answers to his questions. What he did not know then was that I was equally suspicious of him, and any of my fellow-prisoners, for that matter. If I revealed to anyone that I was a special agent, and that information reached the Germans by someone's accidental slip of the tongue, I knew I should be grabbed and shot.

That was the dread that haunted me throughout the whole of my two years at Stalag Luft III. That the Germans would discover that I was not a paratrooper, but a special agent; it would have spelt sudden death for me.

So, I gave Stanford-Tuck the same spiel I had given my Gestapo interrogators in Rome. I was aware that there were one or two gaps in my story, but it could not be helped. I dared not risk being given away to the Nazis. It was not until sometime later that Stanford-Tuck and one or two other fellow-prisoners in authority learned the truth about me. And they guarded my secret as closely as I did myself.

Over the prison camp grapevine, which was always kept humming with gossip and rumour by the arrivals of new prisoners, I had picked up an item which struck me as being vitally important. A man named Waddington, shot down over France, had been provided with food and clothes and contrived to escape capture for a time. Then he had been picked up by the Gestapo and, suspected of being a special agent, was thrown into the notorious Fresnes prison in Paris. Later he had proved that he was a pilot who had baled out, and was sent off to a prisoner-of-war camp.

While in Fresnes, however, the occupant of the cell next to Waddington had tapped a message through to him. This prisoner had given his name as Marc. When this scrap of news reached me, I decided to go to Stanford-Tuck and put my cards on the table. I felt by now complete confidence in him, and the wing-commander, who was our own camp commander. I told them what I really was, and in return asked for further information about Marc. I learned that he had been sentenced to be executed, but Waddington had left Fresnes before the sentence had been carried

out. As a result of my talk with Stanford-Tuck and Day, I was able
to question Waddington closely about the messages Marc had
tapped through to him from the next door cell in Fresnes.

The message which most shook me was one Marc had tapped
out: "Tell Harry he was followed the last time he was in Paris."
This meant nothing to Waddington or to Day or Stanford-Tuck;
but I knew who Harry was. Harry was the code-name of one of
the chaps at Flat No. 10. That he was known to the Gestapo in
Paris was of vital significance. Accordingly, Stanford-Tuck got the
message back to London by code, where it was relayed to MI5,
who in turn passed it on to Flat No. 10.

Marc's vital tip-off arrived too late to save a whole crowd of
our agents in France from being picked up by the Gestapo. What
had happened was that Harry had gone over to Paris to make
contacts with our people there. He had not taken sufficient pre-
cautions, and the Gestapo agent had shadowed him from the
moment he had arrived. Not only did he lead his shadowers from
agent to agent, but a German spy followed him back to London.
Apparently, he made the return journey via Spain, and so the spy
had been able to stick with him all the way.

When, all unsuspecting, he arrived in London, the spy had
tailed Harry to Flat No. 10, and so learned this was the French
Section, British Intelligence headquarters. Now the German agent
was able to photograph everyone arriving at or leaving the flat.
These photographs were sent to the Gestapo in Paris; from now
on the Gestapo knew the identity of our people from Flat No. 10,
even before they arrived in France, and they were picked off like
flies. During my parachute-jumping at Ringway trainee school,
a local cinema manager had been caught taking photographs of
some of the instructors from the school. So, I knew that enemy
spies were operating in England all right.

When Marc's message eventually did reach London via Stalag
Luft III, Sagan, Silesia, the French Section, British Intelligence was
shifted from Flat No. 10 to another part of London.

Early in 1944, during a snow-storm, which raged bitterly for
days on end, I conceived another of my brilliant escape ideas. It
was simply that I should cover myself with a white sheet and so
make myself invisible against the snow. I calculated that I could
cross the no-man's-land, scale the first barbed-wire fence, wrig-
gle through the barbed-wire entanglement, and scale the outer
barbed wire. But when I put it to the escape committee I was told
that I was not the only one who had dreamed this one up. Two
others were planning to escape in this way, and so it was thought
advisable for me not to try mine. Too many chaps nipping across

in white sheets, even in a snow-storm, was likely to lead to the show being given away. As it turned out, the two other prisoners did not go through with their plan, but by that time the snow had stopped and I could not go ahead myself.

The most popular escape plan was to tunnel your way out. During the two years I was in Stalag Luft III more than twenty-five tunnels must have been started. But only one was completely successful, that is the prisoners escaped through it and got clean away, and that was the one constructed by Eric Williams and his two companions as described in his famous book, *The Wooden Horse*. Apart from being one of those who used to vault over the wooden horse, I had nothing to do with this escape. The success of Williams and his two companions, Philpot and Codner, in getting out of Stalag Luft III and staying out, eventually to reach England, created a terrific commotion amongst the German authorities. Several goons, as the camp guards were called, who were held to be responsible for allowing the escape, were sent East to the Russian front as punishment.

Meanwhile, I had begun working with a lot of others on another tunnel, through which we planned to get a couple of hundred of us out. Brickhill, who was to write a book about it, *The Great Escape*, was one of the planners of this attempted escape, which was how Fraser and I came into it. The wooden boards of our bunks were used for shoring up the sides of the entrance to the tunnel. In the end we each of us had only three boards left to sleep on.

We managed to collect bits and pieces with which to make trolleys for getting the sand out of the tunnel as it progressed, inch by inch. Six hundred of us worked on the tunnel. Seventy were selected, those who'd done the most work or could speak German, and 130 more drew names out of the hat. I never actually worked in the tunnel itself.

My job was to help disperse the sand which came out. Little bags of sand were hung under my clothes, and while I walked round the camp I used to allow the sand to trickle, bit by bit, down my trouser-legs. I was one of the 130 who were going out.

The job was completed in the spring of 1944. We waited impatiently for the night when we were to make our escape to fall. As the hour drew near, those of us who would not be going until the end waited in our rooms with our windows slightly open, tensed to hear machine-gun fire in the darkness, or the alarm being raised. I was a long way down the list, in the last fifty or so. There was a bit of a mist, and as it curled round the camp, seventy-six chaps got out of the tunnel and away into the pine forest. As the seventy-seventh poked his head up out of the tunnel-end he was seen by two camp-guards, who happened to be returning from the town at that very moment. They grabbed him and raised the alarm, but the others, waiting their turn in the tunnel, managed to get back to the hut underneath which the entrance-shaft began.

By next morning twenty-five of the seventy-six were rounded up and brought back to the camp and placed in solitary confinement. For two weeks we heard nothing of the others. Then one morning the camp Kommandant ordered our senior officers to assemble in the hut which we used as a theatre. "Never before," the Kommandant began, "have I been ashamed to wear the German uniform."

Then it was learned that every one of the fifty remaining had been caught and shot by the Gestapo. We were all completely overcome with horror. It appeared that many of the fifty had been forced to give themselves up, due to exhaustion and exposure in the bitter weather. Many of them were so badly frost-bitten that they could no longer walk. The Gestapo took them to their headquarters at Görlitz on the River Oder, near the Polish-German frontier. There they shot them. Afterwards, all the bodies were cremated.

The whole ghastly business culminated in an apology from Ribbentrop in Berlin, sent to us at Stalag Luft III. The ashes of the fifty men were flown back to Sagan for a military funeral.

But whatever regrets the Nazis may have expressed for this act of frightfulness, Himmler showed us very little sympathy. Now, instead of the Luftwaffe authorities, it was the Gestapo who supervised the camp. We were warned that any escaped prisoner-of-war caught in a special area would be shot without warning or trial. Of course, the special area was not indicated, so what it boiled down to was that any escaped prisoner caught would be shot out of hand. The reason given for Himmler's measures was that he was convinced Stalag Luft III was a trouble-spot deliberately organized by, and in touch with London, through secret radio-transmitters, and was maintaining contact with anti-Nazi cells in Germany. We even became suspected of having been connected with the bomb-attempt, in July 1944, on Hitler's life. And so, the Gestapo took over, with the S.S. thugs to guard us.

These new goons really were the thugs we had been told so much about. Leather three-quarter coats, grim, ugly faces, they hardly added a touch of gaiety to our cage. What really used to get on our nerves was the way they would suddenly swoop on us in the early hours of the morning. They would clear us out of our rooms while they searched everywhere for whatever we were supposed to be hiding there. We used to get our own back on them a bit by pinching a hat or a pair of field-glasses, or whatever we could lay our hands on from them.

One night, during one of these S.S. swoops, a chap in the room next door asked the guard if he could go to the lavatory. "*Nein*," the guard barked at him. These S.S. guards used to carry their helmets slung from the belts behind them, and on this particular occasion the electric power failed, plunging the camp into darkness. When the lights came on again, the prisoner who had been refused permission to use the lavatory had used the nearest goon's helmet instead. It was very difficult for us, who knew what had happened, to watch the guard go off, quite oblivious of what he was carrying in his helmet, without yelling with laughter.

A good many of the Kriegies, some of whom had been at Stalag Luft III almost from the beginning of the war, had become slightly eccentric. We used to have a batman to every four officers, either an A.C.2 or an Army private, and our chap was a private, who had been captured at Dunkirk. He suffered from an hallucination that he was riding a horse; whenever he came to our room he would go through the actions of dismounting from his horse, and when he left he would mount again and ride off. Several other chaps went about talking to pet parrots which were apparently on their shoulders, or pet monkeys, or who were always whistling their dogs to heel, or giving their pet cat milk.

Another prisoner, a long, lugubrious fighter-pilot, a Scot, who wore a pointed beard, had conceived the idea that he could cheat his captors by reversing the time: that is, by going to bed when everyone else got up, by wearing winter clothes in the summer, and so in the summer evenings he sweated in his thickest clothes and overcoat, and in the winter he froze in shorts and thin socks.

A more tragic case was that of a prisoner who tried to commit suicide by cutting his wrists open during a card-game. He was taken off to our hospital hut; the Germans refused to allow him to be sent to a proper mental hospital, although he was obviously deranged. One day the poor devil managed to get out of his room and on to the hospital hut roof. He was seen by one of the goons from one of the watch-towers, who shot him dead.

Even our own camp doctor, a Frenchman who had been at the camp since the beginning, when he had been captured at the fall of France, became a shade light-headed at times. Once when I went to him for something to fix a chill, he said: "I'm suffering from a chill myself; tell me, what are you doing for yours?"

The doctor used to express his gratitude that at any rate he had no sex-problems among his patients. Not like it had been, he used to tell us, early in the war, when he had been in charge of a camp near Berlin, holding Allied service-women, who had been captured during the French collapse. It seemed that what with their *affaires* with the guards, and the visiting doctors attending them for their various ailments, they drove the German authorities into such a frenzy that in the end they were only too thankful to repatriate the lot.

Contrary to stories I was to hear afterwards about prisoners-of-war, I never encountered any case of homosexuality among those of us at Stalag Luft III. All we worried about was food and when we should be free; we had little physical or nervous energy left for any sexual activity, even if the opportunity had been offered. Some of the chaps who appeared in our amateur theatricals, and had played women's roles, might have given the false impression they were homosexuals. They wore their hair long, one or two of them, and we used to give tea-parties for them at which they would turn up in their stage-clothes. And during rehearsals they used to throw fits of temperament, an "actress" would refuse to appear with this or that actor as "her" leading man.

Even if the inclination had been there, there was no privacy in which homosexuals could indulge themselves. You could not even go to the lavatory privately – the place had no door on it.

Though there were these dramatic, sometimes amusing, as well as tragic events to enliven our days, it was the monotony which, to the majority of us, was so deadly. I kept myself very much to myself after the mass-escape business. I had begun giving French lessons to several fellow-prisoners who passed the time studying languages. I myself was studying for the Oxford and Cambridge examinations for teachers, specially arranged correspondence courses for students who were prisoners-of-war. I had decided that when the war was over I would become a teacher of languages, and so fulfil my schoolboy ambition.

I did, in fact, succeed in passing the examinations, and became entitled to hold the Cambridge and Oxford Higher Certificate for Teaching, but, as it turned out, I made no attempt when the time came to use my qualifications and become a teacher.

I used to spend hours walking round the prison compound, smoking. I was a chain-smoker by then, and even in the pouring rain I would walk and walk, smoking all the time, holding my hand like an umbrella over my cigarette. This walking was to stand me in good stead later, when I was forced to keep walking if I wanted to keep alive. By now my roommates had been doubled in number. The mounting air attacks, now reaching their climax, with thousands of R.A.F., American and Russian planes pounding Germany, meant an ever-increasing flow of prisoners for Stalag Luft III.

Most of us soon got bored with our fellow-prisoners' stories of how they had been shot down, but I was more than bored, I was sickened by the tales of destruction and horror of these terrible air-raids. Naturally airmen spoke of what they had done from their point of view, high above, and did not seem to realize what must have been happening down below as their bombs pulverized their target. Perhaps I felt more strongly about this than anyone else, because I had been bombed and strafed myself. I knew a little bit of what it was like down there.

All the same, it used to puzzle me, the insensitiveness of some of the chaps as they discussed the raids they had been on, the fighters or flak they had encountered, the bomb-loads they had dropped. They spoke of the beautiful bombs; the bigger the bomb the better the job. They talked quite calmly about the first phosphorus-bombs some of them had dropped on Hamburg, how the fires were so intense that the air was burnt up, people came out of the shelters and died like flies, because there was no air to breathe, so that at first the Nazis thought the R.A.F. had been using gas-bombs. When they spoke of these things the chaps did not express any feeling of shame or guilt, even the chaps who had actually dropped the bombs.

It was during this time that mail began to come through from my father and mother, and I learned from her that she prayed for me every day, and that Mass was said on my behalf at the church at Isleworth. I could imagine the candles burning and the incense, and I thought it was all rather ironical. My thoughts went irresistibly to the sort of worshippers at church who, in France, are known as *grenouilles de bénitier,* or frogs of the holy water. Mostly, when Catholics go into church, they cross themselves with the holy water in the bowl on the right-hand side of the church entrance. I knew that many go to church, cross themselves with holy water, and pray without thinking about the prayers they are saying. When my mother wrote to tell me about the Mass that was said for me, that was all I saw in my mind's eye, the *grenouille de bénitier,* who, immediately after the service was over, would forget all that they had been asked to pray for.

And the priest himself was quite possibly thinking of something else, and just saying Mass for me as a matter of course, and through habit. And I tried to reason how it was that such a great and powerful force like the Roman Catholic religion had done so little to stop the war: why the Pope had not excommunicated or threatened to excommunicate Hitler or his Roman Catholic chiefs and advisers.

I knew that if I had written and told my mother all this she would not have understood; I found no one among my fellow-prisoners who could possibly understand what I meant. To whom, or to what could I turn?

As the old year of 1944 began to die, Russian bombers were flying over Sagan. We could hear the drone of their engines in the long nights. While we walked round and round in the snow, we could catch glimpses of refugees straggling through the pine forests. The Russians were drawing nearer and nearer.

As 1945 dawned the straggle of refugees became a steady stream, the noise of bombers more insistent; and then shortly after 23.00 hours on January 26th, 1945, we heard shouts of: "*Aus, aus*" in the darkness. We thought maybe the Russians, whom we knew were advancing towards Sagan, had arrived at last. The goons were milling around excitedly, and told us to collect all our belongings and prepare for a long march.

There was great excitement, as we collected our belongings into sacks and improvised bags. It was snowing very hard and bitterly cold, and our greatest need would be clothing and food. I decided to leave my books and take as much food and cigarettes as I could carry. I pulled out my paillasse-cover which was like a sack, and filled it with cigarettes and food. I wore a leather jacket, which I had bought from an American for twelve bars of chocolate, army trousers, army battledress-tunic. I had a French overcoat which reached to my ankles, and pulled an R.A.F. cap on my head and carried my bundle on my back.

We waited around until 06.00 hours, while we all, guards included, sorted ourselves out, and preparations for our march were completed. We were all so thrilled at the thought of going through the gates we could think and talk of nothing else. But we did take care to leave nothing behind for the Nazis in the way of soap and cigarettes. We put all the cigarettes we could not carry with us into one hut, and then set fire to it; there were millions of cigarettes burnt in there.

They made a wonderful bonfire, lighting up the darkness of that bitter cold morning, and our eager faces shone in the light of the flames.

# Chapter 14

# The Americans

We started that march from Stalag Luft III, fourteen hundred of us, and swarms of goons armed to the teeth, even with machine-guns, came along to keep an eye on us.

We were heading south, though to exactly where we had no idea. But we did not really care since we were out of the camp. It was pitch dark as we set off, no moon at all; only the whiteness of the heavy snow which was reflected in our faces. We all thought that the march would be child's play. We had forgotten that for years most of us had been starved, that our stamina had gone; after a few miles the sacks and bags we carried became heavy, and gradually the chaps began to throw things out, beginning with the heavier things like tins of milk and other concentrated food.

I kept thinking of the refugees who were coming behind us; it would be rather good for them, especially when we were throwing away packets of cigarettes. I had found it was easier to drag my bundle through the snow. Even the guards became tired after a few miles, and we ceased to march four abreast and became a straggled line of weary people. Our ears began to get very blue and we had to stop every so often to massage them to prevent frostbite.

That day we did about fourteen miles, and then we came to a small village called Kunau, and stopped for the night at a farmhouse. The farm buildings had a high wall all around them, with two entrances, both very heavily guarded. We were herded through the first of these entrances.

It seemed to me that our march must end in one of three things: collapse by the roadside, when the S.S. would probably put me out of my misery with a bullet; or the S.S. would grow weary of the whole thing and machine-gun the lot of us; or we should find ourselves in another damned cage. I took a poor view of all these possibilities and decided to escape. It was now or never.

I found two fellow prisoners who had the same idea as myself: Jean Chauvin and the other, Jacques Laurent, both fighter-pilots of the Free French Air Force. Chauvin was from the south, very heavily built and swarthy, aged about twenty-six. Laurent was a young Parisian of about twenty-two, who had been a prisoner for only six weeks. Chauvin had escaped once already, but had been forced to give himself up because of the cold. We had asked quite a number of the others to come with us, but they all refused.

It was a large farm and was worked by French prisoners-of-war. They lived outside the high wall, in a hut which was guarded during the night. But they moved more or less freely to and from their hut and the farm. Our own goons had left us alone inside the farm walls, they were keeping guard outside, so we could speak to the prisoner-of-war workers. One of them, a very young sergeant who had been captured in 1940, was willing to help us. Chauvin and Laurent were also wearing French greatcoats similar to mine, and the sergeant obtained some French caps for us.

There seemed to be no signs of our march that day, and I went to see Stanford-Tuck and told him about our escape plan. He wished me luck, and we waited until darkness fell. Three French workers had agreed to stay behind at the farm while the three of us went out in their place. They told us not to worry about them, they would get out later, they had their proper identification papers, and could make some excuse for their late departure from the farm. They gave us three buckets into which we put our food and cigarettes, and we dressed ourselves to look as much like the French prisoners-of-war as possible.

At the entrance gates the guard on duty was unsuspicious, merely asking us if we were carrying soup in the pails. We said we were and hoped he would not ask for any. My heart was racing, but we passed casually through the gates, speaking French to each other, and unhurriedly followed the wall for thirty yards. It was all we could do not to run for it. I could feel the guard's eyes boring into my back in the darkness, but we restrained ourselves.

At the end of the wall we were met by pre-arrangement by one of the workers, who was to take us to where we were to spend the night. It turned out to be a barn belonging to another smaller farm nearby. Reaching the barn, we went quietly up a ladder into a loft filled with straw. We settled down, but we did not sleep much; we were longing for a cigarette, but dare not smoke with all that straw around us.

In the morning we heard the sound of dogs barking, and we guessed that the guards had spotted our absence, and put dogs on our trail. Our tracks would have been covered up by the snow, which was falling all the time, so the dogs would have very little chance to follow us. About eight o'clock a girl's head appeared at the top of the ladder, and Chauvin spoke to her in German.

She told him she came from the south of Russia and worked on the farm. She was very big and ugly, but she brought us up our breakfast, which was black bread and German sausage.

We spent the entire day in the barn, then in the evening the worker who had brought us there came back and told us to follow him. He led us through the darkness of what seemed to be the village street. We came to a low-built hut, and our guide opened the door. Then we were inside the hut, which was brightly lit and full of French workers. We smelt meat roasting, which was marvellous. It was explained to us that the German guard was supposed to sleep on the premises, but he preferred to slip off and spend the night with a woman in the village. He habitually locked them in the hut at 22.00 hours, and returned early in the morning to let them out again. Chauvin, Laurent and I sat down with the others and tucked into the supper of roast meat, which had been stolen from somewhere by someone, somehow. No questions were asked. It was the first decent meal I had enjoyed since North Africa, two years before.

In the middle of it all, there were sudden heavy footsteps outside; the guard had come back earlier than was expected. The three of us went under the table on our hands and knees. The table was long and narrow, and we could see the door open and the guard's boots come in and halt at the end of the table. The boots remained there a long time, as the guard chatted away. I was sure that he would come and sit down, if he had done so he must have kicked one of us and the game would be up. I could not keep my eyes off his boots.

After what was really only ten minutes, the boots moved away, the door opened and closed, and the guard had gone. We were locked in for the night. The windows of the hut were heavily barred, and we could not break out that way; it would make too much noise, and in any case the workers would have suffered for it afterwards. So, we spent quite a comfortable night where we were, warm, if sleeping restlessly beneath huge red eiderdowns.

As 06.00 hours came, we were told to lie under the eiderdowns and keep still, the guard would not stop very long. It worked all right, we lay nearly suffocated underneath the eiderdowns, while the guard clumped in, chatted again briefly, and then went out. Then the same worker who had brought us to the hut guided us quickly and quietly through the dark village off to our hide-out in the loft. Presently the ugly girl arrived with black bread and sausages for our breakfast.

Chauvin and I noticed the looks Laurent was giving the girl, ugly as she was, and the next day he went off with her to a corner of the barn below. Anything was better than nothing, so long as it was a woman, that was Laurent's motto. The way the girl fussed about him, as a result of his making love to her, was touching. She tried to keep him the best bits of bread and inevitable sausage. Laurent pretended to take them, but he always shared the food with us after she had gone.

We stayed for nearly a fortnight at Kunau waiting for the Russians. We expected their tanks to come through any day; we knew they were on the other bank of the Oder, which was about five miles away from where we were. All day long there were lines of refugees and Russian and Allied prisoners-of-war streaming through the village. Chauvin, Laurent and I watched them through holes in the roof of the barn.

We had hollowed out a cave in the vast mass of straw in the loft, leaving an entrance hole across which we could quickly pull some straw if we heard anyone near and feared discovery. Then one day Laurent left his boots outside the entrance. By chance an old German farmer came up to the loft for some food for his horse. He saw the boots, which were impossible to get in Germany at the time, and took them away. The other two were inside the straw sleeping and I was dozing. I opened my eyes in time to see the old farmer walk off with the boots.

He must have seen us in the straw, and I woke the others and told them what had happened. Before we had time to move the German, the girl and the owner of the farm, a woman of about thirty-five, all arrived up in the loft. The woman, who was a big-boned and dominating blonde and with wide apart light blue eyes, began to interrogate us, and we said we were French prisoners who had run away from the big farm and were just resting in the loft, before moving on. The German wanted to hand us over to the S.S., but the woman said: "*Nein.* This is my farm, I can do as I please."

It was 15.00 hours, and the woman warned us that if we were still there in three hours' time she would hand us over to the S.S. The woman and the German went away; the girl told Laurent she knew another place where he could hide until the Russians came, and Laurent went off with her, with our best wishes.

Chauvin and I talked over our next move. Chauvin decided he, too, would wait for the Russian advance, but I wanted to push on. The Americans were coming up from the west, and I thought I would head in that direction. As darkness approached, and it would soon be the hour for us to clear out, Chauvin left to find the French worker who had taken us to the hut the second night of our stay in the loft. I was left alone.

Suddenly I heard footsteps down in the barn, and a woman's voice called up. It was the woman who owned the farm. The time limit she had given us had not yet arrived. She spoke in German and French, and I answered her as best I could. She put her head over the top of the ladder. Her face seemed very pale in the gloom of the loft. She asked me where the others were. I told her they had gone, I did not say where, and that I was just on my way. "Komm," she said to me. She told me that she would hide me in her farmhouse. She explained that she, herself, would have to move soon, and she would need help. I could help her, the Germans were preparing everyone to evacuate the place in the face of the oncoming Russians.

I went with the woman, she gave me a good meal, with some sort of home-brewed beer to drink. We did not talk much, because it was difficult for us to understand one another, but I kept catching her gaze on me, a speculative look. She was running the farm alone, her husband was on the Eastern Front, she did not know where. She had not seen him for two years. It seemed that the only workers she could get were an odd old man or two and the Russian girl. They all slept in one of the outbuildings.

I wondered how Laurent was getting along with the girl. I asked the woman where I was going to sleep that night. "With me," she said, her pale blue eyes fixed me. "You are an escaped prisoner-of-war," she said. "I know."

I knew that unless I did what she wanted she was quite capable of seeing that the S.S. got me. She fetched a bath full of hot water, and I enjoyed my first bath for ages. I wallowed in it. Then I produced some cigarettes and we smoked over coffee that the woman made. Then, "Komm," she said, and we went to bed. The whole thing was degrading, but I knew, and she knew, that I was in her power. I was not so squeamish that I was not prepared to put up with her animal appetites in order to keep my freedom and my life.

There was plenty of work to do in the day-time, getting ready for the move. But I fed well, and the woman was very pleasant to me. It was a curious relationship, and when I found those strange pale eyes of hers on me, I used to wonder what was going on behind them. Orders to evacuate came through, and I kept out of the way while an S.S. squad came round and poisoned all the cattle and pigs and set fire to every farm in the vicinity. The Russians would find nothing left, only scorched earth, the same as they had left their land before the advancing Nazis.

Just before we moved off, I saw some German cavalry preparing to go back into battle. I was standing on a ridge near the farm and saw the cavalry arrive in the white field below. The Russians were only on the other side of the horizon. I saw the men and horses come back to reform for another attack; I could see the men's sweat-grimed faces, and the horses were steaming in the cold air and nervous. The men wore high riding-boots and no helmets, but the sort of cap the Russians wear.

There were about four or five hundred of them. I suppose they must have been in an attack against Russian cavalry who were trying to cross the Oder. The snow was heavy over the field, and I can still hear the stamping of the horses' feet and the chinking of their harness.

I saw by the expressions on the men's faces that they were wondering if they would ever come back after the next charge, and I felt very sorry for them. It looked so old-fashioned as they set off at full gallop once more, it reminded me of the stories my father had told me of the 1914-18 war.

So, the whole village of Kunau set off; I rode a bicycle beside the farm wagon which the woman was driving. Everything went well, and no one took any notice of me; everybody was too occupied with their own troubles.

The first night we stopped at a farm, where I heard that the chaps from Stalag Luft III had been marched all the way to Bavaria. There was a rumour that Hitler had ordered them all to be shot, but the Luftwaffe had refused to carry out the order. The Germans blamed everything concerning the war on the R.A.F. and the American Air Force; that was the reason for Hitler's order for all airmen to be wiped out.

We set off again next day, but the going now became tough, the wagon's wheels sank into the mud. Once I put my bicycle to one side to give a hand to shift the wagon. When I came back for the bicycle it had gone. The place was full of German soldiers. Travelling was pretty safe for me; I went along with the thousands of refugees. All the time I wore the uniform I had left the camp in, but I had abandoned the greatcoat as it made walking rather cumbersome. I had taken the captain's pips off my battle-dress jacket and put them in my pocket. My clothes were so filthy by now, it required a close look to see that they were khaki. My shoes were wearing out rapidly, already I had a large hole in one. After a short time, I had to give them up altogether, but I kept going on in my bare feet.

All along the way I met French prisoners-of-war, more or less free to do as they liked, who used to take me to their living-quarters and give me a meal and shelter for the night. The next day I would push on.

At one place I stole a woman's bicycle and travelled a few miles on that, but when I got a puncture and left it for a moment to see about getting it mended, it was gone when I came back. But I could not complain. One evening I joined in a game of vingt-et-un with a crowd of Frenchmen, some Poles and Ukrainians. I had five marks on me which Stanford-Tuck had given me at Kunau to help me on my way. I came out of the game with two hundred marks, which I thought was not too bad, since I had never played before.

One of the party did a deal with me, he sold me a pair of German riding-boots for my winnings. They were two sizes too big for me, but my feet were not in too good shape, and the boots would at least be better than tramping barefoot through the snow.

At one time I joined up with an old man, his wife and her mother, a terribly old woman. They were travelling in a horse and cart, which I helped to drive. Early one evening the old grandmother died. There was a rule which forbade refugees from burying their dead in the towns or villages through which they were passing, they had to be buried a certain distance away, in the fields. So, the old husband and his wife wrapped the grandmother in a sheet and put her in the cart, intending to bury her next morning. They were also carrying in the cart a pig which had been freshly killed, from which, time to time, they cut pieces of meat to cook and eat. The pig was also wrapped in a sheet, and in the night someone came to steal it, and went off with the old woman instead. They must have had a shock when they discovered their mistake.

One night I slept in a barn, which I learned later had been used by a pack of poor devils the Nazis had been shifting from some concentration camp. During the following day and evening, I felt an increasing irritation all over my back. Eventually I could stand it no longer, and I took off my shirt and vest and found I was crawling with lice. I remembered the previous night I had spent in the barn; it was obvious that it was there that I had picked up the lice. I was very scared that I might have been infected with typhus, but I could not throw my uniform away, it was all I had, and fresh clothes would be impossible to obtain. The same morning, I stopped at a village and found a wash-house with a boiler. I put all my clothes in there and that was the last I saw of the lice.

It was early February by the time I neared Dresden. I had travelled all the way with different groups of refugees and slave-workers, and no one had suspected me of being anything other than a French worker. I arrived at Dresden in the evening, a few hours after the Americans had bombed it. Dresden had never been bombed during the whole of the war; the Allied air forces used to pass over the city on their way to Berlin. During this time something like three million refugees passed through the city, and this particular day the place was simply swollen with old men, women and children. The Fortresses came over as usual, everyone merely looking up with the thought that Berlin was in for another raid. Then down came block-busters and chaos and destruction, horror and terror hit the unsuspecting thousands of human beings. When I arrived, Dresden was still on fire, ambulances were tearing around incessantly. I had seen all along the aftermath of Allied bombing, the ruins and devastation everywhere, but never had I actually seen what the immediate results were like.

I hung around in a sort of trance of horror, and then at about 22.00 hours the roar of the bombers could be heard again. Loudspeakers all over the place were calling: "*Hah-gumt, hah-gumt, flieger bomber.*" This time they were R.A.F. planes. I saw them reflected in the flames of the still burning city, the aircraft flew so low. Then I ducked into the entrance of the nearest air-raid bunker. High explosives and phosphorous bombs rained down. The raid only lasted about an hour, but to me it seemed like a hundred years. In the shelter children were crying, and some went out of their minds, women were throwing themselves on the ground, screaming prayers to God. There were only women, children and old men in the shelter.

When the all-clear sounded I came out, shaking all over with fright, upon the most ghastly scene I have ever witnessed. Everywhere people were running about in flames – if only a little of the phosphorus touched you, you went up into a sheet of fire. The screaming was like a lot of wild animals. It was like one of those horrific pictures you see of the end of the world.

The Nazis admitted that a total of three hundred and fifty thousand people lost their lives. The first raid had wiped out forty-five thousand people, the greatest loss of life from any single raid during the war, except the atom-bomb raids on Hiroshima and Nagasaki. But I think that there must have been even more killed. The town was so jam-packed, thousands of people could never have been accounted for. Most of the dead which littered the streets were burned beyond recognition. All that was left of Dresden was a skeleton, a few walls standing and smoke-clouds blotting out the sky. The fires could not be put out, there was no one and nothing to put them out with, and long after the raid ended I could still hear people yelling as they burned to death, trapped in basements and cellars.

I did not know if the bombers would come again, but even if they did not come I could not bear to stay there anymore. I headed out of the place.

Next morning, I arrived at a village about twenty miles away. I was told by some of the villagers how they had read their newspapers that night in the street by the light of the flames of Dresden. They looked at me as if I was some miracle-man, when I told them I had not long come from there. I was now able to feel safe about my lack of identity-papers; I need only explain that I had been in Dresden during the raid, and it would be taken for granted that I had lost everything I possessed.

The Russians and the Americans were drawing closer and closer, with the refugees in the middle, so there was little point in going on. I had lost a lot of weight on the road, I had to eat when I could get food, otherwise I just went without. By now I was getting weak, my bones were beginning to stick through my skin, I felt I could play a tune on them. I must get food.

I thought I would get work on a farm. That way I could scrounge some food, and hang on until the Americans, who were supposed to be pretty near, had arrived. The French workers at Kunau who had helped me to escape told me that whenever I tried to get work I must say I was a farmworker, otherwise I should be sent to a factory, where I would starve to death, or be bombed.

I set off on the road again, and found a farm, which, it transpired, belonged to an actor. There were a dozen other French workers there, also two Russian women employed as slave-labour. In the farmhouse lived the owner, his wife and daughter, and a little German maidservant, aged about fifteen.

It was a big farm. All the workers slept and ate in the barns and stables. The actor-farmer took a dislike to me pretty soon; he put me on to a fortnight's job, clearing a huge manure-heap with my bare hands. He took a delight in watching me, and giving me a rap with his thick, heavy walking-stick whenever he passed. Then I got the job of potato-planting, back-breaking work. I was sent out with the two Russian girls on this. I found out that they had been officers in the Russian medical corps. One was very dark, the other blonde, and they both took a poor view of our boss. Come the Russians, they used to say, and they would cut his throat.

It was April, the weather was lovely, the skies blue and the sun shining. American planes were flying over all the time. Surely the

Americans must arrive any day now? But there was still the River Elbe, a few miles to the west, to cross. Both the Russian girls were good-looking in a heavy, square-faced fashion. Soon we became friendly, they used to sing sad songs to me; and then when we were sure we were safe from spying eyes, the blonde would lie down in the shallow ditch alongside the hedge with me. The brunette would keep watch. Another time the brunette and I would get down into the ditch, while the blonde kept watch. That was how we made love under that blue April sky, with the drone of Flying Fortresses overhead.

But it was the little maidservant who was so very sweet to me. The food was terrible, black bread, watery soup; nothing else much. But the girl, Erica her name was, used to steal food from the farmhouse, and bring it to me when no one was about. Then one day the actor-farmer caught her just as she was coming to me, where I was working in a corner of the potato-field. I heard her scream out, and saw the boss setting about her with his damned walking-stick. I rushed up, and as he turned to ward off my attack, I tried my commando stuff on him.

He yelled as I kicked him in the crutch, and then I wrenched the stick from him. The girl ran for it, as I bashed his own walking-stick over his head. Even when he collapsed under my blows, I kept hitting at him with the stick. I did not stop until I began reeling about from exhaustion, and found myself hitting him across his back and buttocks.

He was dead. I dropped the stick and ran off across the fields. I ran on and on like an automaton. Darkness fell, but still I kept on, jogging, running, walking. That night I did not stop at all, I kept moving all the time. Through the fields and woods. I headed for the west, and just hoped and hoped I would run into the Americans, while I had the strength to go on. The actor-farmer's death would soon be discovered; I was terrified that the S.S. would catch up with me. That would mean the finish, kaput for me.

After three days I came on to a road approaching a biggish town. I passed the gates of a concentration camp and noticed they were wide open. No one was there. Then I was amazed to see Nazi soldiers entering the town, taking their belts off. I could not grasp what was happening, my main thought was that I had to get food no matter the risk – I had not eaten since I left the farm, only grass and some leaves.

As I walked through the outskirts of the town, the streets were all cobbled, I was feeling absolutely light-headed, stupid, and asked someone where I was. Magdeburg, I was told. Then I saw coming out of a shop, their arms filled with bottles, two American soldiers. The Americans were there. I half-ran, half-stumbled up to them and explained who I was. I was incoherent, I had no means of identifying myself, but they grinned understandingly, while the tears ran down my face.

I was safe at last.

# Chapter 15

# Back In Britain

Magdeburg is on the left bank of the River Elbe, and had surrendered that day – it was 18th April, 1945 – to an American force which had pushed across the river. Then a Russian force had arrived from the East, with the result that the respective commanding officers did not know who should occupy the city. I turned up in the middle of this confusion, and the American command at once suggested to the Russians that I took on temporarily the job of looking after Madgeburg, while the Russians and Americans decided the matter. To both commands I, being a British Army captain (and no one doubted my word in this respect), was neutral, so to say, and so it was that, within an hour of my arrival, I was made boss of the city.

An escaped prisoner-of-war in danger at any moment of being caught and shot by the S.S. one minute, the next, in a position of supreme power over a Nazi city of over a quarter-million people, plus the thousands of surrendering Nazi soldiers streaming into the place. It was like coming out of a nightmare into a dream. But it was real enough.

Leaving me to take over, the Americans pulled out and back about thirty miles, assuring that they would keep up a regular supply of food to the city; while the Russians also pulled back for about the same distance. That was how the situation was left, the Russians and Americans awaiting instructions from the high-ups as to who did what.

I promptly set up my headquarters in the town hall, fixing myself living accommodation there, and set about organizing a sort of military police force to deal with the refugees, and the surrendering Nazis, all of whom were milling around in confusion, throwing the whole place into a state of chaos. I gathered together a bunch of French prisoners-of-war (who were now no longer prisoners-of-war), issued them with German rifles, minus ammunition, since there was none to be found, and sent them off to keep order. I put up my Captain's pips again, later I added the American equivalent in rank, so there would be no question of my authority, found a decent pair of boots, stuck two revolvers into my belt, and sent for the local burgomaster and the chief of police.

I had seen that among the refugees were several thousand people, old men, women and children, from the nearby concentration camp, whose gates I had noticed open on my way to the city. I told the burgomaster and the police-chief to order all the shops to supply the concentration camp refugees, many of whom were collapsing in the streets, emaciated and in rags, with free food and clothing. At first the burgomaster refused. I took my revolver out of my belt. I knew how to deal with Germans all right.

"Obey my orders to the letter," I barked at him, "or I'll blow your brains out here and now." The burgomaster offered no more argument. Both he and the police-chief shook like reeds in the breeze every time I sent for them, I made them feel so nervous.

The Nazi soldiers presented a bit of a problem at first. Then I shoved all the high-ranking officers into the local jail, and told the rank-and-file they could either clear out and head west to the Americans, who would take care of them, or they could stick around and wait for the Russians. It acted like a charm, the vast majority of them preferred the prospect of being in American hands, and they cleared out.

One of the concentration camp refugees was a young girl who was picked up by my military police as a suspected spy. She had been among a batch of half-dead, half-crazy souls I had ordered to be put into a block of flats – the German tenants I had kicked out. Because she was not so emaciated, so deathly in appearance as the rest of the refugees, it was thought that she might be a Nazi agent who was hoping to escape notice amongst this mob from the concentration camp.

They brought her to me. She was dark-haired, pale and very striking-looking. She did look a little plumper than the others I had seen from that hellish place. She was Polish, she said, but we each managed to make ourselves understood.

Her age?

Eighteen.

How long in the camp?

Three years. She had been taken there with her father and mother.

Where were they?

She had seen them put into the gas-chambers. What the S.S. guards used to do was to make batches of the prisoners strip stark naked, then force them to run round the camp. Then the prisoners would be halted, and those who were perspiring would be dragged off to the showers. The showers were what they called the gas-chambers. They did this on Sunday mornings, whenever the camp began to get too full.

How did she escape being taken to the showers?

She had been put to work in the camp-hospital. She had come out of it alive, because she had shown a natural aptitude for nursing. And because she had always made herself agreeable to the S.S. guards in turn whose fancy she caught.

Her name was Luba, she said. It meant love.

Luba told me a lot more about her experiences in the concentration camp, unmentionable things, all in her flat, unemotional voice. She offered to come and help keep my quarters clean, attend to my laundry. She was all alone, she said, she liked company. She liked me. She offered herself to me. Unemotionally, in the same flat voice she had used to tell me about the camp. I sent her back to the block of flats, and spent the rest of the day trying to forget the things she had told me.

Where had God been during all this? It was this that I kept asking myself; and what I had learned from Luba, which I knew to be a mere drop in the ocean of horror and agony of human suffering the years of war had brought upon the world, only confirmed my conviction that there was no God. My mind used to reel beneath the stored-up recollections of what I had endured, of what I had witnessed, and of the acts I had myself committed these past few years. That night in Dresden, when innocent human creatures ignited into living torches screamed through the streets; these human skeletons crawling round the block of flats like a lot of mutilated flies. I did not know, understand, perhaps it was because I had not had the time in which to learn, that I might have found God within my own heart. It did not occur to me that perhaps the peace I sought was all the time close enough, if only I chose to reach out for it.

For two weeks I lived like a lord, all the food, the wine and cognac I needed, and bossed Magdeburg: the burgomaster and the chief of police bowing and scraping to me every morning. In the city, where foreigners had been those to be downtrodden and despised, I now saw the position reversed. I did my best to see that everything possible was done for the refugees, the ex-prisoners-of-war, for whom I got extra food brought in from the outlying villages, while the people of Magdeburg went without, meekly obeying the orders I handed out.

On my fifteenth day at Magdeburg the Russians took over, and I rode over on a motor-bicycle which had once belonged to an S.S. guard, whom I had seen beaten and kicked to death by several of my military police, to the Americans. The road was crowded with refugees, the sort of human chaos I was becoming used to witnessing; and now I was edging my way through thousands of the same sort of walking skeletons I had encountered at Magdeburg.

When I reached the American headquarters, I learned that several concentration camps had been opened, and more were in the process of being cleared. I was given a smart new uniform in exchange for my dirty motley and asked to give a hand with the job.

The very first camp I went to with the Americans, we caught some of the S.S. guards. First, we gave them the job of helping to bury the dead, and there were plenty of corpses strewn around to keep them busy. I then commanded an escort which took the S.S. men to another concentration camp which had been reserved specially for them. There were some Luftwaffe and Nazi officer types there too, and they were forced to watch the way the Americans handled the S.S. personnel. Stripped to the waist, the S.S. men stood on their toes, their arms stretched above their heads, and every time their heels touched the ground or their arms dropped there was an American in charge to hit them across the jaw with a rifle-butt. They were made to stand like that for hours.

Next, they were set about digging trenches for latrines, being led to believe that they were digging their own graves. I rejoiced for Luba's sake to see the abject terror on the white, sweat-glistening faces of these thugs as they shovelled out the earth, fully believing that their last hour had come.

While I was at another concentration camp, one that had held mostly Hungarian Jews, an American sergeant came into the office, where I was having a smoke. He was a young Hungarian Jew, who had gone over to the States when he was about seventeen or eighteen, leaving his family behind. During the war he had lost touch with his family, and now he had just learned from some Hungarians released from the concentration camp that his father and mother had been amongst those captives who were sent to the gas-chambers. He asked me if I should like to be present when he interrogated one of the chief S.S. guards who had been caught in the camp, and who was in the next hut. But I had seen enough of the way the Americans treated the S.S. When the sergeant went out of the office, I turned up the radio that was playing as loudly as I could. But I could still hear the S.S. man next door screaming with pain above the blaring of the radio.

I stayed with the Americans until the beginning of May. Then I heard that a repatriation camp had been set up at Lübeck, where the Allied ex-prisoners-of-war were being looked after. There was a job there I could do, helping to sort out the men and getting

them on their way home. Besides, it was about time I began thinking of getting home myself. I had not written to my family, or any
friends, since Stalag Luft III, several months ago. So, no one knew
what had happened to me, where I was, or anything. For reasons
which I could not explain to myself, I made no effort to try to get
in touch with anybody now, not even Father and Mother. I just
did nothing about it. I kept telling myself I would wait until I got
back to England before I let anyone know where I was, or that I
was alive, even.

I reported to the American headquarters at Lübeck, and was
asked if I would mind living in a block of flats belonging to
the barracks where the Allied troops were now packed like sardines. All the flats, except the one I was to occupy, were still
occupied by S.S. officers' wives. It was a luxury block; I had
a sumptuously furnished lounge and two bedrooms, kitchen
and wonderful bathroom, all to myself. I had hardly been in the
flat ten minutes before there was a ring at the front door. It was
one of the German wives. She spoke a little English, and was
extremely friendly, wanted to know if there was anything she
could do for me. I had before me pictures of what I had seen in
the concentration camps run by monsters such as her husband
was, and I was cold and sharp-voiced. I did not ask her into the
flat. After a few moments she realized she was not wanted and
she went. But she gave me a little smile, as if to say she understood the way I felt. She was aged about thirty, well-fed looking
and smartly dressed.

This was early afternoon, and I went back to headquarters to
work with some American officers, who were available, on the
problem of getting the Allied chaps on their way home. It was
a colossal task: there was such a mix-up of troops, British and
overseas men, including Indians, French and Hungarians. And
there were few of them who were in a quiet frame of mind. Being
cooped up in barracks was not their idea of a good time; they
wanted either to get out and go home, or grab for themselves
food, wine and women.

The Americans had fixed a curfew, so that only those on official
business, such as the troops patrolling the town, were allowed out
of doors. In any case there was not much of the place left. Apart
from being a garrison town, Lübeck had been a vital port for the
Nazis, handling troops and supplies for the Russian front. It had
been terribly devastated by the R.A.F.; almost all the wonderful
ancient buildings had been razed to the ground. I was subject to
curfew as much as anyone else. So, I was back at my flat by 19.00
hours, while it was still daylight.

I became terribly bored alone in the flat, and after I had cooked myself some supper and knocked back several drinks – I had supplied myself well with food and liquor – I felt I should go mad with the monotony. What was there for me to do, except think? Let my mind fill with thoughts and memories I wanted to forget? In the end I recalled the German woman in her flat only a few doors away. She had mentioned to me her flat number. Presently I found myself ringing at her door, asking her if there was anything I could do for her. Was she all right for food? Did she need a drink, or cigarettes?

The woman at once asked me in and introduced me to her sister-in-law. There was some drink, and they had food. I supplied the cigarettes. Then three or four more women came in, all wives of S.S. men, and all telling me that their husbands were fighting on the Eastern Front, what there was left of it, from the Nazis' viewpoint. None of their husbands, according to all these women, had been in charge of any concentration camps. None of the women knew anything about the concentration camps. They all smiled at me disbelievingly when I told them what I had seen. They remained unconvinced, they were sure that I was merely spreading atrocity stories against the Germans.

Then a tall, dark woman, aged about twenty-eight, came in with a portable radio, and we all listened to and danced to the dance music, and my glass was always full, and there were good things to eat, and I danced a lot with the dark woman, who kept pressing herself very close to me, and smiled at me with her sexy, dark, slanting eyes. She was married to an officer of very high rank, she told me. Her name was Greta. Oh, yes, she had heard all about the concentration camps from her husband, though, of course, he had not had anything to do with them. But I forgot all such things while we danced and drank and laughed.

At about 03.00 hours the party ended. Greta asked me quite blatantly to come to her flat and go to bed with her. I would have done so, there and then, only I remembered Luba and her account of how she had seen her parents taken off to the gas-chambers; I remembered that Greta was the wife of an S.S. thug. And so, I pretended to take her offer as a joke; I said I would rather borrow her portable radio for the rest of the night to soothe me to sleep. Greta thought she had embarrassed me by asking me to go to bed with her before all the others. She played up to me and lent me her radio, and off I went back to my own flat.

The next evening, when I got back to my flat, the blonde woman whom I had known first called. She said she had a message for me from Greta. Would I remember to return the radio to her? I guessed that Greta would be waiting for me, alone, and I made up my mind that I would not stay with her for a moment longer than was polite. I had some supper, started knocking back some drinks, and then I took the radio along to Greta's flat.

She was alone all right. She was wearing a filmy *négligé*-affair, and I knew that she had not got a stitch on underneath. She was very casual and asked me to have a drink. The flat was much more luxuriously furnished than the other woman's flat, with thick carpets and soft lighting. She put the radio on for me and gave me some magazines to look at. They were a few months old. "I have a little ironing I must do," she said. "But you can stay here and make yourself at home." She went into the bedroom, but left the door open. I could hear her moving around, sometimes she would sing to the music over the radio.

I lounged back in an easy-chair and listened to the music. I forgot my earlier determination to go as soon as I had returned the radio. Presently Greta called out to me: "Come and tell me, give me your opinion of these." I stood in the doorway of the bedroom. She was holding up a pair of black lace panties; there were other flimsy underclothes lying around, which she had been ironing with a little electric iron. The bedroom was warm, and beyond her the bedclothes on the wide bed were spread out invitingly, and heavy perfume filled the air. It was all very obvious, but I did not care about that as Greta murmured something about how ironing made her feel warm, and she began undoing her *négligé*.

There was a photo by the bedside.

Her husband in his black S.S. officer's uniform.

He was smiling at me, and I bashed my fist at it and knocked it to the floor.

Greta smiled at me; he was a long way away, she told me; I did not need to worry about him.

A few days later five R.A.F. officers turned up at the barracks, and I thought it would be a good idea if I invited them to share my flat. From that evening on, it was one long round of parties. There were six men to twelve officers' wives. We provided cigarettes, some drink, some food. They provided the rest of the food, drink, and themselves. A pretty hectic time was had by all.

On 8th May, news reached us that it was over, so far as Europe was concerned. Our soldiers' farewell to World War II was the occasion for our biggest celebration of all. I gave the party in my flat, but it spread to nearly every flat in the block. We all crowded into Greta's flat to hear King George speak over the radio. All the women stood on their heads when the King had finished, while the six of us stood to attention and shouted: "Down with Hitler, up with Mr. Churchill." The women joined in.

A week went by: my job at the barracks all day, and parties at my flat, or the flats of the officers' wives all night. And then it was all over; one morning we got news that the five R.A.F. types and I were going home. A lorry called to take us to the airfield, first stop Brussels; then England, home and beauty. The women we had enjoyed such good times with crowded round us as we climbed into the lorry. Greta clung to me as if she would never let me go, the tears streamed down her cheeks. Then we were off, and waving *auf wiedersehn.*

And I did not even look back. I did not give a damn for Greta or any of those women. All I wanted to do was to get back to London.

We reached Brussels in the afternoon, the end-of-the-war celebrations were still going on. My five companions and I joined in. I do not remember what happened during that brief stay of mine in Brussels. I have a hazy picture of a very pretty brunette whom I picked up in some restaurant; then there was dancing and drinking in a night-club in the Rue Neuve. The drinks, champagne mostly, flowed as if someone had turned on a tap. I came round and it was early morning; I was in a jeep between two British military policemen who were driving me to the airport. I got there just in time to catch the plane to England.

We landed at an airfield in Surrey. It was a bright Sunday morning, and as we got out of the aircraft on to the tarmac, I took deep gulps of good old English air. It was an age since I had last breathed it from the troopship bound for North Africa. Buses were waiting at the airfield to take us to a big house two or three miles distant. There, everything was laid on for us.

Breakfast, X-ray examination, delousing with D.D.T., hot bath, and, since I was still wearing my American outfit, I was given a nice new uniform; someone even sewed my captain's pips up for me. By lunchtime I was all set, complete with ration-cards, clothing coupons, identification papers, and £10 in cash.

I caught a train to London. On the way I tried to make excuses to myself for still not having written my parents. I had not written to anyone to say that I was alive and safe. I pretended to myself that I had all along wanted to give my father and mother a surprise. I sat like someone in a dream, watching the green fields, the woods and houses with their little gardens go past. When I got out of the train at Waterloo I was still in a dazed state; it seemed incredible to be back where I had started from two years ago, alive and kicking, without even a scratch. I thought of what had happened to so many of my friends. Men like March-Phillips and Leon, Appleyard, and those I had known in Stalag Luft III. All of them killed.

I had been one of the lucky ones. That was what I thought then.

So, my thoughts churned round my head as my taxi whisked me through London, out to Isleworth. For some reason or other, I cannot think why, I stopped the taxi on the corner of the street about twenty yards from my parents' house. It was a typical Sunday afternoon, quiet and somnolent, as if all the occupants of the houses I passed were enjoying their afternoon snooze. I passed a dog lazily scratching himself as he sat in the middle of the pavement.

My footsteps slowed as I neared the house; I could feel my muscles tense, my heart race a little, as I braced myself to open the iron gate and walk up the short path to the front door. The gate did not squeak, and I recalled how Father always used to oil the hinges, because, if the gate squeaked, it got on Mother's nerves. It was like coming back to a different world.

Half-way up the path I paused, there was no sound within. No one was at the window. I guessed that they would both be in the sitting-room at the back, Father lying back in his chair, the Sunday newspapers spread over his knees, asleep. Mother would be nodding over her Bible.

I stood at the door, my hand on the door-handle to turn it and go in, my mouth was opened to call out that it was I. Somehow, I could not turn the handle. Supposing, I asked myself, the shock upset Mother? Quietly I pushed open the flap of the letter-box and tried to look through. But I could not see properly. The hall was dim, I saw the vague outline of the hall-stand, with coats hanging on it. Then I heard the sounds of someone moving about, in the kitchen, getting tea ready.

There was a dreadful choking sensation in my throat. I let the letter-box flap close quietly. I turned away and went out of the little gate.

I walked quickly along the street, back the way I had come.

# Chapter 16

# Far East Assignment

I walked for quite a way before I came to a tube station and, only half-thinking what I was doing, bought a ticket and got on to the train.

A little later I found myself walking in the direction of Flat No. 10, and it was not until I was half-way down the street that I remembered that British Intelligence (French Section) had been transferred to another part of London, as a result of the Harry business.

All the way in the tube I had kept telling myself that the reason I had run away from Isleworth was that I had been afraid my sudden appearance at home would shock my Mother and upset her. I reassured myself I would think of some way of going back there, so that my parents would be prepared for my arrival.

Not only had my old headquarters been moved, but there were new faces in place of those I had known. The major was no longer boss – instead a tall, fair-haired, typical army type, who had become well-known for his secret service work in Occupied France, was in charge. Those chaps I did know were very glad to see me. It seemed that I had been placed on the list of Stalag Luft III prisoner-of-war reported missing, and I was presumed to be dead. I learned that Roger had been killed. I was also told that Lieutenant B., who had seen me through my special agent training from my first day at Flat No. 10, had been killed as a result of a stupid accident on the day France was liberated; his Sten gun had gone off accidentally, killing him outright. I also heard that Major D. had been killed in a car smash.

There was plenty of talk at the new headquarters about my being sent to the Far East, but first I was told to get myself really fit again, and go for a prolonged leave. I was told that I could expect to have nearly a thousand pounds to my credit in the bank. This was a small fortune to me, and my immediate reaction to the news was that I would be able to have a whale of a good time for the next few weeks. After that I would have a job in the Far East. Headquarters advised me that they would get in touch with me; meantime I was just to take it easy and wait until I was sent for.

I was not to know that Hiroshima and Nagasaki were soon to put paid to any prospects of my continuing my career as a special agent in the Far East.

Blissfully unaware of what the future held in store, I determined to enjoy myself all I could until I had to report for duty again. The feeling completely possessed me now that Life had nothing left for me, except to continue the job I had been doing. It was all I could do, all I had been trained for, this lone-wolf fighting and killing. This was a job I knew I could handle. This was a job that fitted in with my new-found philosophy of eat, drink and be merry for tomorrow we die.

It was against this confusion of mind that I tried to face up to the problem of my parents. It seemed pretty certain that they had given me up for dead, as no doubt had all of my other relatives and friends both in England and in France. What was to be gained by Father and Mother learning the truth about me? I, who was already lost to them and their way of thinking. My Mother's faith only sickened me, and I knew that if I had to spend much time in her company, I should not be able to restrain my feelings, and I should pour my scorn and cynicism upon her and her belief in the goodness of God. It seemed to me that she would rather think me dead, so long as I had died believing in what she believed, than alive without faith.

Somehow, the idea of starting life afresh, for that was how I saw it, without the responsibility of family or relatives to cramp my style, made a strong appeal to me. I saw it as a sort of escape. I did not know then that I could not escape from myself.

I was aged only twenty, but I felt older, aeons older, than most people around me. I felt youthful only in the company of my superior officers, or men who had witnessed more of the war than I had. These attributes comprised the yardstick by which I measured up life.

I decided to put up at the Norfolk Hotel, while I sorted myself out in preparation for my Far East assignment, which I anticipated in the very near future. The hotel was just the same as ever: still the genteel atmosphere, the marble and gilt and plush, the quiet little restaurant. It was here that I had dinner that evening, at a table to myself. There was no one I knew staying there. Afterwards I had a couple of drinks at the pub opposite, and then my footsteps led me, as they had done so often in the past, down to the Embankment.

Presently, I found myself wandering along the Strand; I had turned up some side street, and I kept on walking. Down Whitehall through the dusk, to pause outside the door in the familiar grey building by the entrance to the Horse Guards Parade. In my nostrils was the smell of the stables, and memories of that room came back to me. I could see it again as it was the first time I went there, to join Appleyard and March-Phillips, the faces of young men, eager and excited in the haze of tobacco-smoke. I could hear their buzz of conversation.

I remembered Graham Hayes, with his thick hair and moustache full of vitality and giving the impression of great depths of strength. Graham, who had been cold-bloodedly murdered in Fresnes. The date of his death had been, as I had learned over the grapevine in Stalag Luft III, July 13th, 1943. The same day on which Appleyard himself had died so mysteriously.

Amongst all the news I had been given that afternoon was the story, as far as it was known up to that date, of the flight upon which Appleyard set out and which had ended so fatally. It was just before the Allied landing in Sicily, and Appleyard was planning an airborne drop at a spot north of Randazzo, with the idea of capturing and holding a strategic bridge in advance of the Allies' forces.

On the night of the 12th July, Appleyard decided to fly over the spot in order to learn beforehand where it would be best for his dozen or so paratroopers to land. He went in an Albemarle, PMP 1446, ahead of the aircraft carrying his paratroopers. He left the airfield at 22.00 hours and was due back at 01.00 hours the next day. The course both aircraft took from North Africa was over the Mediterranean till just before Taormine, when they turned sharply inland to Randazzo.

The operation was concluded. Appleyard's handful of paratroopers made a successful drop. They were the last to see PMP 1466 turn away. The terrain was hilly, but the night was brilliantly clear, and Appleyard's pilot very experienced. There was little enemy flak going up and very few enemy aircraft about; but neither Appleyard nor the pilot, or plane was ever seen again.

Other ghosts began to crowd me as I continued along Whitehall. March-Phillips: I remember the sound-proofed room in the flat at Flat No. 10, and March-Phillips, the elder of the two men waiting for me, with his military moustache, and black coat and striped tropsers, and the bowler hat and umbrella he carried; and how he and the other chap, Appleyard, whose eyes had been such a bright blue and full of excitement, had told me of what they were planning against the Nazi outposts on the Channel coast. I could hear D.'s voice again, when I told him I had got the job with March-Phillips and Appleyard: "You're damned lucky. They're two of the very best; you wanted excitement, you'll get it with them." March-Phillips, to whom I had last waved goodbye that September night in 1942, as he and Appleyard and the rest of them were setting off for the Cherbourg raid from which he was never to return.

There had been Leon, with his gay laugh and soft tones of the South, who had died with such nonchalant courage at the Nazi naval training school at Toulon. There was D., whom I had last seen in Algiers, but who I was remembering now when we had dined together at the Norfolk Hotel before I went off on the abortive plane trip over France in 1942. And I thought of Marc, and how he and Edouard and I had enjoyed such good times together drinking at the Ritz, and ending up at the Savoy Grill, with the crowd dancing to Carroll Gibbons and his band, and the alluring girls he had painted on the walls of the mess at the shooting-lodge at Fort William. Like Graham Hayes, Marc had been done to death at Fresnes.

Where were they all now? That brave company of chaps who had been so gay and vital, so full of life and courage, where were they? Now they were no more than ghosts, whose faces hung about me in the darkness of the June night as I walked on and on; and whose voices were elusive whispers against the rumble of London's traffic.

It was about nine o'clock when I suddenly felt desperately tired, my knees were aching. I began to think about returning to my hotel and bed and a good night's rest. My wanderings had taken me as far as South Kensington, and I was only a few yards from the tube station. I was so tired, and my mind so confused with the thoughts and memories that kept churning round inside it, that I could not think of the nearest station to the Norfolk Hotel. I had to explain to the man in the ticket office, who gave me a ticket to the Temple.

At some stop, after I had changed on to another line for the Temple, I noticed out of the corner of my eye a chap in the uniform of a lieutenant get in and sit opposite me. I did not turn to look at him at first; then, when I did, I was shocked by his appearance. His cheeks were sunken, beneath his cap I could see that his head was shaved. And then as I stared at him, our eyes met, and he stared back hard at me. His mouth opened as I suddenly got up and grabbed his hand. "Marc!" I yelled. "What the devil are you doing here? I've just been told you're dead."

It was Marc sure enough. And he was equally surprised to see me. The last time he had called at Flat No. 10 they had told him that I was dead. We were both filled with amazement to see each other alive. I told him how I had heard of him in Stalag Luft III, through Waddington, who had been next door to him at Fresnes, and how I had got hold of the message about Harry.

Marc said, yes, it had been him in the cell next to Waddington. He had been caught by the Gestapo in Paris, he said, while radioing a message to London. After Fresnes, he had been sent off to Belsen concentration camp, where he had been kept for two years. Every day he had expected to be shot; the only reason the Nazi camp bosses had kept him alive was that they admired his artistic talents, and one after another of them got him to paint their portraits and those of their women. One Nazi gave him the job of painting his girlfriend in the nude. "I did a full-size picture of her," and his emaciated face creased in his old grin; "that was the only thing about being in a concentration camp I enjoyed. I made the job last as long as I could."

As the American force which was to liberate Belsen drew nearer, the camp bosses crowded more and more prisoners into the gas chambers; but Marc and three others managed to hide, and were saved. He was on his way now, he said, to join an American who had been in Belsen with him. They were having drinks at the Regent Palace Hotel. Marc asked me to go along with him.

By mistake we got out at Leicester Square, and so, on our way to the Regent Palace, I took Marc into a pub. It was crowded, and as we were trying to shove our way to the bar, we stood for a moment next to a couple of airborne types. Suddenly, for no reason at all that we could grasp, one of them pulled out a revolver and shot his companion dead. We did not wait to get our drinks, but beat it out of the pub as fast as we could.

The American, when we found him in the Regent Palace, was already having to hold on to the bar to keep himself upright, but it did not seem to interfere with his enthusiasm for more drinks. From there we went to several bars; I had a hazy recollection of some night-club place in a cellar, people packed in it like sardines, and so dark that we kept calling for the waiter to shine a torch on the bacon-and-eggs we were eating in a corner. I do not remember getting back to the Norfolk Hotel. Curiously enough that was the last time I saw Marc. I never knew what happened to him afterwards.

But there were plenty of other drinking companions to keep me company, most of them chaps I had known in Stalag Luft III, during the next few months. I stayed in London all the time, keeping my room at the Norfolk Hotel, but spending most of my time at parties at the Dorchester, and the usual night-clubs.

During all this time I was tormented by the knowledge, niggling at the back of my mind, that I had done nothing about my parents. Continually I kept telling myself that I would plan to let Father and Mother know that I was safe and alive, but always, when it came to making a decision, I would put it off till the next day, or next week.

Sometimes when I wandered along Piccadilly or Oxford Street, as I often did in the afternoons, I would see someone in the crowd, a man I thought was Father, or a woman who looked as if she might be Mother. But it never was either of them. Even if it had been, should I have made myself known? I know that my first impulse was to turn away or hide my face. I never did meet anyone who knew my parents or any relatives. But this was probably because I spent most of my time in big hotels or night-clubs, always with a crowd of service chaps.

Even if anyone I knew had bumped into me, it was doubtful if they would have recognized me at first. Not only was I wearing my uniform with my captain's pips up, but my figure had filled out; no one would have believed that I was only a youngster of twenty. I wore the same air as that of many of my companions, who after all were only a few years older than I, but who looked like, and gave the impression that they were mature men who had been around.

One night early in August, while I was in a Piccadilly bar waiting for the arrival of some chaps with whom I was going to a party, a sudden longing to see my Father and Mother filled me again. It was so overwhelming that I put down my drink, hurried out into the street, and took a taxi for Isleworth. I had no plan in my head, no idea of how I could turn up at home without risking causing my parents, especially Mother, a tremendous shock. I had acted upon an impulse. I decided I would chance it, something would happen when I got there, I told myself, that would make it all right.

As I had done before, I stopped the taxi on the corner of the street, a short distance from the house. It was now about half-past nine, still daylight, and the evening warm and quiet. My footsteps echoed loudly on the pavement as I neared the house. The same emotions that had overcome me on the previous occasion began to reach down to the very roots of my being once more. As my pace slackened, my heart began banging, and I had to brace myself to open the iron gate, and walk up the path to the front door. I did not pause, but set my teeth, and walked straight up to the door-bell. As I pressed the button I heard the sounds of someone beyond the hall. Then the bell jarred the sounds of movement to a sudden stop.

The footsteps came hurrying along the hall. They were not slow footsteps; they were not the footsteps of someone middle-aged; they were quick footsteps. The door opened, and a girl, aged about fifteen, stood there, staring at me questioningly.

"They're not here anymore," she said, after I had found my voice and asked for my parents. "They went away about a week ago; they went to France, I think."

I always had a newspaper with my breakfast, which I invariably ate late, in bed, though I barely even glanced at the headlines. One morning on August 7th, 1945, about a week after my visit to the house at Isleworth, I could not miss the great black headlines which glared at me from my breakfast tray. The Americans had dropped the atom bomb on Hiroshima.

The news did not make a great impact on me at that moment. Not because I was woolly-minded as a result of the inevitable party I had been on the night before, but because it seemed to me to be merely another sample of man's inhumanity to man. I remembered that night in Dresden, and this Hiroshima business looked like another grim business of the same kind.

I did not realize it meant the end of the war in the Far East.

It never occurred to me that in two or three weeks' time I should be out of the special service.

The prospect of being out of a job never entered my head.

# Chapter 17

# 'A Certain Crisis In My Life'

A short while after the first atom bomb on Hiroshima, followed by the Nagasaki holocaust, and Japan's capitulation, I reported at headquarters for the last time. The war was over. The special service was being disbanded, there was no longer a job for me. I was bowler-hatted. I was out of work. It took me months for it to sink in that chaps like me were no longer necessary.

At the end of that time I had got through every penny I had. Wine and women. Eat, drink and be merry, for tomorrow we may be on the dole.

One evening I was down to literally my last few shillings, and I wondered vaguely how I was going to get money. I was coming out of a café off Shaftesbury Avenue when someone behind me called out my name.

It was Emile.

He looked rather scruffy, but I was glad to see him. One of the first things I noticed as my money began to run out was how my pals no longer seemed to be around anymore. All the girls I had known, the soft, white-limbed girls, so ready with caresses: there was not one of them that I had set eyes on for weeks.

I had not seen Emile since Lisbon. It was good to talk to him again. I went back into the café with him. He was just the same, boasting as ever about his amours, and telling me what he was going to do when things started going his way again. It seemed that he, too, had thought his job with the French Section would last for ever. He, too, had gone through his money as easily as a hot knife going through butter.

But he had been luckier than I in one respect. His vaunted virility had won him the undying love of a little waitress, a French girl. When he found himself broke, Yvonne had taken him into the two-roomed flat in Paddington she had. It happened that the girl she had been sharing it with had moved to another part of London to work. So, there was room for Emile. When he heard how I was fixed he said at once that I must come and stay with him. Yvonne would not mind. In the end I agreed; I was thankful to find someone whom I knew and who had not forgotten the old days when we had once been comrades-in-arms.

For over a year I shared the flat with Emile and Yvonne. She was a dark, plump little thing who adored Emile and would have willingly thrown herself under a bus if it would do him any good. Because I was Emile's friend, someone who had fought in the same war, that was good enough for her.

My first night there the nightmares started. I had gone to bed at about midnight, and suddenly I was reliving all the horror of sudden death and destruction in the darkness of a Cherbourg beach; once again I was emptying my Sten gun into bunches of Nazi figures; only in my nightmare, of course, the menacing figures kept reappearing no matter how much I fired at them. Then I would relive the hazards of the North Africa desert, my hand-to-hand knife fight with the Arab spy, the look in the eyes as I shot him, of the father of the little Arab boy.

Everything that I had ever encountered of cruel destruction I experienced all over again. Only now everything was distorted and swollen to terrifying dimensions. I would awake screaming and sweating. The first time it happened I found Emile struggling with me on the bed, which was made up for me on a camp-bed in the sitting-room. Emile and Yvonne slept in the bedroom. We laughed about it together, after it was all over; it reminded Emile of the nightmare he had suffered after his disastrous first and only parachute-jump.

But the next night the nightmare came again.

And the next night.

For a month or more I suffered these nightmares. Emile and Yvonne were marvellously kind to me. Yvonne made me go and see a local doctor, but there was not much it seemed he could do for me, beyond giving me sleeping-pills, which had no effect, so that I gave up going to him. After the month the nightmares wore off a bit. I would go two or three nights without any bad dreams, then back they would come, and for night after successive night I would wake up screaming and fighting.

The nightmares began to take on a sort of pattern. In a way it was always the same dreams, that is to say, the same incidents occurred. But sometimes one happening would be in the background, sometimes in the foreground. But always, like a strong thread holding the beads of experience together, were my Father and Mother. When a dream would mount in a frenzy of horror as I went back to Le Chabanais in Marseilles and dragged the body of the Gestapo man through the labyrinth of cellars and passages, the corpse growing enormous, then suddenly dwindling until I felt myself dragging a tiny doll, there at the end of it all would be, not the parents of the agent who owned the Café de la Jobette, but Father and Mother.

Soon I found that Emile and I were living on Yvonne's earnings as a waitress, which amounted to only several pounds a week. Like me, Emile, although he was much older than I, was only beginning to realize that there was no longer any room in the world for lone-wolf fighters willing to take on any job, no matter how hazardous. Like me, Emile had no idea how to go about getting employment of a more normal kind. Before the war he had been an actor and stunt-man in films. Work had been difficult enough to get in the pre-war days, when he was young and had built up contacts with agents and producers, or people who knew him. Now he did not know anyone who could help him. He was new to everyone, everyone was new to him.

Emile turned to any sort of job anywhere. Being of a somewhat artistic bent, he would, for instance, paint a shop-owner's shop-front. But he would get sick of it half-way through, and having obtained some of the money in advance, which was soon spent, he would fail to turn up to finish the work. Or he would put in a week or two as a handyman-commissionaire at some Soho drinking club, until it got raided, or closed up of its own volition.

Always Emile was the optimist. Somehow, somewhere, something would click, he would boast, and we would all hit the jackpot. One thing about him, he always included me in his rosy dreams. He looked after me like a father. I began to grow more and more depressed – one result of sleeping so badly. Once a nightmare hit me I could not go to sleep again: fear of the nightmare returning held me back from sleep. Stabbing a man face to face, or creeping upon him from behind out of the darkness, silently and swiftly, these scenes I could not endure again in evil dreams. I would lie awake, eyelids stiff, eyes staring up into the gloom, jerking up suddenly as I felt myself drifting off into sleep which I dreaded would not be sleep, but only being dragged down into an abyss of horror.

My parents seemed farther off than ever before. I used often to think about them, back at the village on the Somme, and I used to concoct all sorts of foolish plans by which I could return to them, quite naturally and easily, without causing any alarm. I would be there, with Mother and Father again, and everything would be as it used to be when I was a schoolboy. But, of course, I did nothing about it. It was always the big step I must make tomorrow, or next week.

Yvonne tried to help me most of all to make up my mind to reach my family. She felt dreadfully about my parents believing I was dead, when all the time I was alive. But over me hung this dreadful mental and physical lethargy; this lassitude of heart and mind. I was like a creature without a soul. No doubt had I placed myself in the hands of those who were caring for war-shocked cases my story today would be different. But I was not long out of my teens; I was haunted and bedevilled by death and chaos; I had been a schoolboy who had been pitched headlong into a storm of blood and destruction, who in the space of five years had experienced what most men who live their full span of years would never know.

Emile did not possess the wisdom necessary to set his own feet along a secure and straight path, let alone direct me the way I should go.

It was Yvonne who saved me from trying to gas myself.

It seems ironic that I, who had come through the war without a scratch, should attempt to do what the enemy had failed to do. The flat had a gas-oven in the rabbit-hutch of a kitchen. It was a shilling-in-the-slot affair. One day I had been dismally trailing along Edgware Road and through the back streets. It was a grey afternoon in the autumn of 1947, and as I passed a greengrocer's shop, I spotted a shilling glinting under the edge of the shop front. I picked it up, and walked on without anyone noticing, and arrived back at the flat. It was empty.

I cannot remember exactly what my actions were after I had closed the front door behind me. Some violent depression must have taken control of me. Whatever I did, I did completely unconsciously, driven by some inner compulsion. I can remember clearly thinking about March-Phillips and Appleyard and the others who had died. I can remember a longing to be with them, to be uplifted by their inspirations as I had been what seemed to be long, long ago.

I can remember the strong smell of escaping gas and my being awoken out of nothingness by someone shaking me violently. It was Yvonne, and she dragged me away from the gas oven, and I had a vague idea of her opening the kitchen window. I could hear her voice urging me to wake up as she helped me into the bedroom, where I collapsed on to the bed. By now the flat was flooded with fresh air streaming in from all the windows, and after I had been sick, I began to feel better.

By an extraordinary chance Yvonne had come home from the café where she worked, unexpectedly, about a quarter of an hour after I had put the shilling I had found into the gas meter. I had shut the kitchen door and window tight, turned on all the gas-taps, and lain down with my head inside the oven. If it had not been for Yvonne, suffering a bad attack of migraine, which had forced her to give up working that afternoon, I must have died.

When Emile came back later that evening he was terribly upset by what had happened. He and Yvonne tried to get me to explain why I had attempted to gas myself, but I could not tell them. I did not know myself. I just felt thankful that I had not succeeded in what I had tried to do.

By my suicide attempt I had reached a certain crisis in my life. The next two or three days I tried to decide what I was going to do with my future. It seemed to me that I had become an unfair responsibility for Emile and Yvonne. I determined to find some-where to live on my own. But in order to do that I had to earn money; I had to find work.

I did not tell the others what I had in my mind, except that I intended to start looking for a job. I knew it would have to be some sort of manual work. Obviously in the mental state I was in, combined with my general down-and-out appearance, it would be hopeless to try and obtain any kind of employment as a teacher. Even if I had been offered such a job I could not have taken it on. I could not have applied myself to it.

After over two weeks wandering around London, in the end the best I could do was to land myself at the Strand Corner House washing dishes. I was paid four pounds ten shillings a week. It was through Yvonne's suggestion that I got the job.

At first, passing the front of the Strand Corner House on my way to the employees' entrance, my mind used to go back to those days in 1941, when I was training to be parachuted into Occupied France, and I remembered the little waitress from Swansea who used to serve me with coffee. I wondered vaguely if she was still working there. But I did not take the trouble to find out.

Sometimes I was on the night shift, sometimes the day shift. I waited until I had drawn two weeks' salary, and then I left five pounds with a farewell note at the flat. I explained to Emile and Yvonne that I felt I was too much of a burden for them, and that I was going to get a room on my own and try to stand on my own feet.

I packed my few belongings into an old attaché-case. I had long ago sold all my clothes, except for those that I stood up in, and the few valuables I had ever possessed. I had already found a room for myself in another part of Paddington, but I did not leave my address. I asked Emile and Yvonne not to try and get

in touch with me at the place where I was working. As soon as I
felt like it, I said, I would find them again and we could all have
a celebration.

My job at the Strand Corner House brought me into contact
with several chaps who had been through tough times during the
war. I worked on the Salad Bowl floor, and nearly everyone wash-
ing-up in the kitchen on this floor was either a Polish General,
a captain or someone who had been of high rank in the Polish
Army. Even the women kitchen-hands numbered a lot of Poles
who had served as officers in the women's fighting services. One
chap, who spent all his time washing the kitchen floors, had been
a general; he was very bald with a round face, and tackled his
work quite cheerfully, without, it seemed, any regrets for the old
days. Another man, quite young, had been a lieutenant-colonel
during the war, though before Hitler had arrived he had been a
lawyer in Warsaw. His job was polishing the silver.

That Salad Bowl kitchen became quite a club for misfits like
myself, who no longer had any reason for fighting and killing,
whose services as professional lone-wolf soldiers were no longer
required. As we worked we talked in French or broken English
about the days that had gone and would never come again. We
stood over vast sinks, and before the huge conveyor-belts which
went round the kitchen, bearing plates and knives and forks to
be dried. One of us would take the knives, another the forks, and
so on.

I was a kitchen-hand for several weeks, and then I was promoted to working the goods-lift at an increase of a pound a week
in salary. I shared the running of the lift with a round-shoul-
dered little Austrian Jew. He was about thirty-five, the son of a
Viennese doctor, and he had himself been studying medicine in
Vienna until 1938, when he had got out into Italy. He had finally
landed up in England and joined the British Army. We called him
Fritzie; he knew all the answers, and he and I had a wonderful
time together working that goods-lift.

Some of the food that was served in the Salad Bowl was brought
from the main kitchens at Hammersmith, already cooked. It only
needed to be warmed up in the restaurant kitchen, and it was
then ready to serve. Our job on the lift was to take the food up as
it arrived to the different floors. Once or twice a day Fritzie and
I used to shove a small table and a couple of chairs into the lift.
Then we would stop between two floors, select the food from the
stuff we were carrying, and sit down and enjoy a good meal.

There was a loudspeaker in the lift, over which would come
the voices at different floors shouting for us. But we would ignore

all interruptions until we had finished our meal, and then we would operate the lift again, pretending that there had been a breakdown. During the time that Fritzie and I worked the goods-lift we ate marvellously. I must say the food was really excellent, and I was putting on weight. However, after several months at the job Fritzie left, or was sacked, and the new chap who came to work with me was not the same type. A little while later I found the monotony unendurable and walked out.

This was the pattern my life was to take during the years to come. Getting a job, any kind of job, for a few weeks, or a few months, for a few pounds' pay. Night-work at a milk bottling firm near St. John's Wood; working as a night-porter at a factory in the suburbs. Once I got a job at Barkers in Kensington in the bakery; I stuck it for six months, starting late at night and finishing early next morning, and earning over seven pounds a week. I was always getting burnt, but I quite enjoyed the job at first.

I preferred working at night and sleeping in the daytime, since I found that the recurring nightmares troubled me less when I slept during the day. It was much more comforting to awake out of a terror-filled dream to find it was daylight, than waking up in the middle of the night and darkness. Even so, the nightmares resulted in my having frequently to change my room where I lived. The landlady would complain that my shouting and screaming before I woke up used to upset other tenants.

One job I got was that of house-decorating. I had been unable to find any work for several weeks after quitting my last job, and then when I was absolutely desperate I met one of the Poles I had known at the Strand Corner House. He told me of a man who let rooms in a big house in Maida Vale, who wanted the whole place decorated from top to bottom, but could not find anyone to take on the work at what he considered to be a reasonable price. If I went over there and spun him a yarn, the Pole said, I might get the job. I explained that I had never done anything like that before. "That doesn't matter," my friend replied, "all you want is some paint and a brush."

I was desperate enough to try anything. I saw the landlord, and talked glibly enough to satisfy him that I was sufficiently experienced in house decoration. It was an enormous house of five storeys, and was divided up into a total of twenty-seven rooms, plus bathrooms, one to each floor, and a large basement kitchen. The landlord wanted all the ceilings distempered, all the walls repapered, and fresh paintwork everywhere. He offered me three shillings an hour and a room in the house that was vacant, which I could have rent-free.

I took on the job. All of six months it was before I had finished, working five days a week, eight hours a day. At first I got myself and everything in a frightful mess, but I soon began to get the hang of things, and did not do at all a bad job. At any rate the landlord was quite pleased.

After this I was out of work for a few weeks, until I found myself a porter at a sausage manufacturer on Hammersmith Way.

The drift from job to job continued.

I reached suicidal depths on two occasions; it was a kind of inner compulsion, and the feeling that only by joining my old comrades, dead and free, could I myself find release from the burden of living.

Towards the end of 1953 my nightmares were recurring less frequently. The memories of Appleyard, March-Phillips and the others were becoming faded. My whole being was invaded with an apathetic cynicism. I was spending all my earnings as fast as I got them on drink and, as and when I found them, women. Most of the women I found in pubs, waiting to be picked up; or even a cheap prostitute would serve.

It was through a prostitute that I went with several times, and who was not quite so tough as the others, that I heard of a job going at a club near Old Compton Street. It was a sort of door-keeper and chucker-out job. The club was a cellar, and the water-closet was continually overflowing. It was part of my miscellaneous duties to keep it working. After a while I got fed-up and moved to a similar job at another club farther along the street, but the water-closet worked all right there.

Now I was becoming part of the riff-raff of Soho. Dope addicts, ponces, tricksters and tarts, perverts and down-and-outs of every description; these were the denizens of the underworld in which I lived and breathed. Many times, I was invited to become a partner in some shady enterprise. House-breaking; a tout for a call-girl set-up; peddling dope; or luring unsuspecting seekers after thrills to so-called Black Magic parties.

But I steered clear of all that. I was not interested in the vast amount of loot which I was told I would pick up. I was not interested in anything, except forgetfulness.

I made no friends. I made no home for myself. I merely moved from one cheap backroom to another as the fancy took me. The clothes I stood up in were my only sartorial requirements. Sometimes I shaved, sometimes I did not bother to. I washed when it occurred to me to do so; I had not seen the inside of a bathroom for several years. I ate when I felt like it, my interest in food was nil. I still preferred doing a night job to working during the day; I was haunted by the fear that the nightmares would start up again.

It was the life of an automaton.

I became ill with jaundice early in February, 1955, but I did not give up my job at the drinking dive where I was working. I hardly ate anything at all during this illness, sometimes I had to cling to the walls to keep myself upright. It was Rita, who was a *habituée* of the club, who found me early one morning, trying to walk back to my room. I was reeling like a drunk along the pavement, lurching against the wall and trying not to fall to the ground.

Rita was half-sozzled, her ponce had been sent to prison that day, and perhaps, because she was feeling so wretchedly sorry for herself, she took pity on me and helped me to stagger back to the backroom where she lived.

That was the beginning of my association with Rita.

I think we stayed together as long as we did because I never pestered her to make love to her. Rita was as cold as ice, she hated sexual intercourse, except with Tommy.

It was after I had been with Rita for about six months. I was sitting in a café behind the Casino Theatre, it was approaching five o'clock in the afternoon. Through the steamy windows the street was growing dark, chilly rain threatened. The café was beginning to fill up. I drank off the cup of tea over which I had been brooding the past hour, and got up to go. I stood by the counter, near the door, and I was just paying for my tea when I felt a hand on my shoulder. I turned round sharply. The man facing me was round-faced, with fair hair and wearing glasses. He wore a black coat and white collar of a priest and carried a black trilby. He spoke to me in French: "Jacques, what are you doing here?"

His tone was empty of surprise, it was as if we had met the day before. "I was just going, Andre," I said, and I answered him in the same tone. I made as if to shake his hand off my shoulder, but his grip tightened a little. It was firm and yet somehow comforting, and I let it remain. "I might ask you the same question," I said. "What are you doing here?"

"We are in the way of people coming in," he said, as the door from the street kept opening and people crowded into the cafe. Still with his hand on my shoulder he put down some money for the cup of tea he had been drinking, and we went out of the café. We walked along silently for a little while, my thoughts flying back over the years to the days when the man at my side and I had gone to school together. We said very little to each other, Andre and I, as we walked in the direction of Leicester Square.

Just monosyllables about the cold, dampness of the evening, and how crowded Soho was.

It was strange, that, for I was remembering Andre from the time we had spent together before the war at my home on the Somme. We had not seen each other since then. Even then, though only in his teens, he was determined to become a priest, and of all the youngsters I knew with the same idea in mind, Andre was the one I had felt instinctively who was sincere, and who would mature into a dedicated man. We had been quite good friends during our school-days at Amiens. Then, during those few months before my coming to England to study, our friendship had become stronger. Despite my increasing scepticism, Andre had remained undismayed, his burning sincerity and belief that by becoming a priest he could do good had remained unaltered.

He was Father Andre now. I found myself outside the Church of Notre Dame de France, off Leicester Square. I had passed it many times; it had been badly bombed and I had noticed casually that it was slowly being rebuilt. Andre came to a door, and he opened it, and led me up some gloomy stairs. We passed the first floor, which he told me was the library, and on the second floor I found myself in a little flat, which is for the priest at the church. Andre was staying there while on his visit to London. He had come over to London for the purpose of visiting the French Youth Clubs. He had made the journey several times, he said, since the war.

The sitting-room was dark, the furnishing old-fashioned and rather depressing. I sat down while Andre took off his coat and put on his soutane. He moved about slowly as if his shoulders were bowed beneath some great weight. He seemed much older than his years. I knew he could be no more than twenty-eight or twenty-nine; we had been about the same age at school. We talked conversationally, and his eyes behind his glasses, which glinted now and again as they caught the light through the windows, were still calm with the little smile that I knew of old.

He did not mention anything about Suzanne, he just went on to explain that he always wandered round Soho whenever he came to London. I said something about the extraordinary coincidence of our meeting. He looked at me with that faint smile, and I guessed what he was thinking. Our meeting had not been coincidental, he was thinking, but had been ordained by God.

"The extraordinary thing is," he said, "that I was not a bit surprised to see you. All of us at home had long since assumed that you were dead. You had last been heard of at the prisoner-of-war camp in Silesia. That must be ten years ago. There was something about how you had been on the march from the camp, and then you had disappeared. It seemed that quite a lot of your comrades disappeared on that march. Some were found again. Some were dead, some were alive. But you were among several who were never fully accounted for."

"I had nothing to go home for," I said. "I tried to return to my parents, but I could not."

He nodded understandingly. It was just as if we were back in the old days, talking about religion as we used to. I began to tell him a little of what had happened to me during the war. I began to argue that what I had gone through had taken so great a toll of my spiritual resources that, when it was all over, my psychological make-up was irreparably corroded.

He listened as the gloom of the evening grew more shadowed. When my voice trailed off, when I groped for words with which to try and explain the workings of my mind, the reasons for my actions, Andre made no attempt to help me out. Instead, I found myself listening to him, talking about a monastery near Amiens. It had been used as a school for children, and I myself had attended there as a boy.

Now, Andre was telling me, the school had been moved elsewhere, and the monastery had been taken over by laymen, who helped the priests in their work. It was something new in the Roman Catholic Church, Andre said. It was run by a priest under the direction of the Bishop of Amiens. Usually the priest in charge would be one who came there for rest. It was known as the Order of St. Riquier.

I was remembering the monastery very clearly as Andre talked about it, and the work that was being done there by the laymen, going into the villages round about and helping to teach the children. I was remembering the huge wall all around, which shut off the monastery from the rest of the world. There were the gardens and many old fruit trees. There was the long corridor leading from the refectory to the chapel, where the monks said their rosaries. I could see again in my mind's eye the trees in the courtyard, which had been the school playground when I was there as a boy. St. Riquier was several hundred years old, and there used to be stories passed round among us, about how, underneath the monastery, stretched amazing catacombs, where the monks had hidden in times of war and invading armies.

Andre's voice broke into my musings. "At St. Riquier a man could rest," he said to me. "He could just relax, wear any old clothes, and gradually find himself working in the gardens, or if he wanted to, on the farm. The monastery is rather proud of being self-supporting."

I sensed what was in his mind. "I have given up God," I said.

Andre looked at me, and though I could not see his expression in the shadows, I imagined the smile of understanding on his round face. "Because you have given up God," he said, "does not mean that He has given you up."

Involuntarily a picture came to my mind of myself as I might be at St. Riquier. I could see myself working on the farm there, I could imagine the peace of the place behind the old high walls, away from the world. Out of the deepening shadows of the room Andre's voice came to me again:

"I could help you about seeing your parents again," Andre said. "Together we would think up some way of your return from the dead, so that it would not shock them. Your mother could not stand any upset." I looked at him quickly. "She has been ill," he said. "Oh, she is better now, but she had a stroke. Not a very severe one. And she is recovering."

"I long to see her," I found myself saying.

"I am going back tomorrow," Andre said.

"You know that I passed my teaching exams when I was in Stalag Luft III," I said. "I wrote and told Father and Mother about it." Andre nodded. "If I became … if things were different," I said, "perhaps I could start teaching?"

Had the wheel come round the full circle? Was I really going back home? Was I really returning, like a boy home from school, to my parents, to the place of my boyhood, to my relatives and old friends?

Andre came down the dark stairs with me. We stood at the door, the roar of Leicester Square in our ears, the glare of the lights blotting out the night sky above. For the first time since I had come back to London, the noise seemed to be unendurable. I had not noticed it before, but now it seemed to be deafening. I muttered something about it to Andre.

"You may find a little quiet from the noise there in the Church of Notre Dame de France," Andre said. "It was badly bombed, but work is being done on it. Anyway, there is a chapel under the church. You could pray there, and come back, and we will make plans for tomorrow's journey."

I could sense him still at the door, watching me, his eyes gentle and quiet behind his spectacles, as I turned towards the entrance to the church.

# Index